YOUR WRITING MATTERS

© 2021 by Colleen M. Story. All rights reserved.

No part of this book may be reproduced in any form or by any electronic or mechanical means, including information storage and retrieval systems, without written permission in writing from the publisher or author except by a reviewer, who may quote brief passages in a review.

Although every precaution has been taken to verify the accuracy of the information contained herein, including Internet addresses, the author and publisher assume no responsibility for any errors or omissions. Further, the publisher does not have any control over and does not assume any responsibility for author or third-party websites or their content.

No liability is assumed for damages that may result from the use of information contained within. The author does not dispense medical advice or prescribe the use of any technique as a form of treatment for physical, emotional, or medical problems without the advice of a physician, either directly or indirectly. The intent of the author is only to offer information of a general nature to help you in your quest for physical, emotional, and creative well-being. In the event you use any of the information in this book for yourself, the author and the publisher assume no responsibility for your actions.

Books may be ordered through booksellers or by contacting the publisher at:

Midchannel Press
P.O. Box 52133
Idaho Falls, ID 83402 www.midchannelpress.com
Email: publisher@midchannelpress.com

To receive a free weekly email newsletter delivering tips and updates about putting the power of *you* behind your best creative life, register directly at www.writingandwellness.com/newsletter.

Cover Design: Damonza.com

ISBN 13: 978-0-9990991-4-8 (Paperback edition)
ISBN 13: 978-0-9990991-5-5 (eBook edition)

Library-of-Congress Control Number: 2021905166

First Edition: June 2021, printed in the U.S.A.

Decide to embrace
your true identity as a writer.

YOUR WRITING MATTERS

HOW TO BANISH SELF-DOUBT, TRUST YOURSELF, AND GO THE DISTANCE

COLLEEN M. STORY

MIDCHANNEL PRESS

Also by Colleen M. Story

FICTION

Rise of the Sidenah

Loreena's Gift

Coming Soon: *The Beached Ones*

NONFICTION

Overwhelmed Writer Rescue

Writer Get Noticed!

For more information, please see:

colleenmstory.com

writingandwellness.com

Contents

Introduction	ix
A Note to the Reader	xv

Why Writers Doubt Themselves

1. Decide To Be a Writer	3
2. How to Put the Question of Talent to Rest	15
3. The Alluring Traps of Money and Fame	27
4. Writing as Part of Your Life's Purpose	45
5. If Not Money and Fame, Then What?	63

The Many Benefits of Writing

6. Why Can't We Just Write for Fun?	79
7. Writing to Heal	93
8. Writing to Escape	105
9. Writing to Discover the Truth	115
10. Writing to Release Secrets	125
11. Writing to Boost Brainpower	135
12. Writing to Know Your True Self	145

Make the Big Decision

13. When Writing is Not the Best Choice	159
14. Your World Without Writing	173
15. Embrace the Life of a Writer	187
16. The Reason Why You Write	197

Appendices

Note from the Author	203
Recommended Reading	205
Featured Authors	209
References	217
Acknowledgments	235
About the Author	237

Introduction

My name is Colleen M. Story, and I'm a writer.

If that sounds like the first step in a recovery program, it's probably because it kind of is. It took me years to be able to say those words out loud: I'm a writer. For a good chunk of the 1990s and beyond, I wrote short stories and novels without telling anyone. I couldn't admit it, mainly because I wasn't gaining from my writing the one thing I knew society valued most of all: money.

Eli Cook, assistant professor of history at the University of Haifa, wrote in *The Atlantic*, "By the early 21st century, American society's top priority became its bottom line, [and] net worth became synonymous with self-worth...."

My writing wasn't making money. I had no proof that the time I was spending on it was worthwhile, so I hid it away like a dirty little secret. It wasn't until I got a corporate job as a copywriter that I could finally lift my head and admit I was a writer, because at that point I had a salary to go along with it. So when people asked me what I did for a living, I could finally say, "I'm a writer. Here's my card."

But inside, I still felt I was cheating—or even lying—because corporate writing wasn't "real" writing to me. I joked with my family that I was writing words people read in the bathroom. The back of the shampoo bottle—that is what I wrote. Ditto for the small print on the moisturizing cream. And let's not forget the copy in the skincare catalog: "Rescue dehydrated, stressed-out skin. Apply this creamy, luxurious mask, wait 10 minutes, then rinse. You'll notice smoother, softer, healthier-looking skin—immediately!" Gets you right there, doesn't it?

Of course, many of my projects were more serious than that—research-based writing on heart disease, for example. But I still didn't feel it was "real" writing. To me, real writing meant storytelling, which I continued to do on the side. But very few people knew about it.

It was many years later when I learned I wasn't alone. I've interviewed over 300 writers on my motivational blog, Writing and Wellness, and spoken to many more at writing conferences and other literary events. Almost every single one of these bona fide writers struggled (or continues to struggle) to truly identify as a writer, particularly when not making money from it.

Our culture doesn't help us, either. In the words of Rodney Dangerfield, we writers don't get no respect—unless we have the success that can be measured in terms of money or notoriety. You may have made the mistake of admitting out loud that you are a writer, then quickly learned it's best to keep that bit of information under your hat. Often the second after you mention it, people skeptically narrow their eyes and begin that familiar interrogation: "Oh, have you written any books I might know?"

I wonder why no other artist has to endure this question. People will ask painters what medium they use or musicians what instrument they play. But writers must undergo "the test." If the other person hasn't heard of you, the implication is that you're not a real writer.

"Any books I might know?" The question is moot, as if the person had heard of your books, they'd likely recognize your name as that of the author's. But we writers dutifully answer something about our obscure titles and watch the listener's eyes go flat as they fake their impressed smiles and nod uncomfortably.

This whole humiliating, torturous exchange doesn't happen with any other profession. Mention you're a banker, and you'll never hear anyone say, "Oh, granted any loans I might have heard about?" Tell someone you're a doctor, and they don't ask, "Managed any illnesses I might be familiar with? Pandemics, maybe?" People assume these other professions are real because they have critical value—as in a salary—attached to them. Writers, on the other hand, have to hit it big before they're granted the same respect.

This may not seem like such a big deal to someone on the outside, but it bothers us a lot. Way down deep, we *believe* what this whole exchange implies: Unless our writing has made us rich, famous, or at least somewhat well-known, we aren't really writers, no matter how many hours a day we're compelled to get our stories down on paper.

One of the things we're taught while we're growing up is that society values results and that the monetary ones are most admired and respected. As kids, we were praised for being creative and imaginative. But as grown-ups, we are hit with the reality that what matters is not creativity for creativity's sake, but rather creativity that translates into income. When it doesn't, it's considered an indulgence, a daydream, and—perhaps the greatest insult—a hobby.

In a 2016 study published in *The Journal of Social Psychology*, scientists reported that millennials pursuing higher education in the United States were more motivated by making money than previous generations were. Compared to about 55 percent of boomers who felt the purpose of higher education was to prepare them to make money, about 71 percent of millennials felt the same way. The quest for knowledge and self-development has been supplanted with the quest for a paycheck.

What is this doing to us? Nothing good, if we believe the research. Studies show that Americans are growing less happy overall. Data from the General Social Survey, a public opinion research project, showed that the number of people who said they were not too happy increased by 50 percent between 1990 and 2018. The latest United Nations' World Happiness Report found that overall life satisfaction in the United States fell between 2007 and 2018, landing our country in eighteenth place behind others like Canada, Denmark, Australia, and Ireland.

It's not because we're earning less money. Incomes per person have risen about three times since 1960, but measured happiness failed to rise at all. Per capita GDP (gross domestic product) continues to increase while happiness decreases. This can be traced to several reasons, but some studies point to the fact that we're linking our self-worth too closely to our net worth. Lora Park and colleagues found that the people who more closely attached their self-worth to their financial success engaged in more social comparisons, experienced more stress and anxiety, and felt less autonomy than those who didn't, regardless of their economic status.

In another similar study performed in China, researchers found that a growing number of people link individual success with making money and tend to value money and other outside rewards over intrinsic rewards like relationships, community, or personal development. When analyzing how this trend affected people's well-being, these scientists discovered that those who picked income as an important value were significantly less satisfied with their incomes, even at higher levels.

Indeed, many studies show that focusing on any type of external or extrinsic reward will never instill the same true sense of happiness that focusing on internal rewards will. Therefore, caring about the meaning and impact of our work rather than the financial rewards is the best way for any of us to achieve happiness. The kicker is that a side benefit of this is often financial success!

This brings me back to writing. Sometimes writers ask me questions like these:

- Am I wasting my time?
- What if I don't have the talent?
- What if I never get published?
- What if my books don't sell?
- What if I never make money from my work?

These questions illustrate that we're all facing one serious problem: We're not valuing our creative contributions. It's easy to blame society because if society values creativity for creativity's sake, they sure have a poor way of showing it. But blaming society won't help us feel better. Only changing how we think and feel will.

When I leave this earth, I already know my books will be among the accomplishments I'll be most proud of. They will probably never make me rich and famous, but they are worthwhile achievements. What about you? Will you feel the same way?

I know you've cracked open this book for many of the reasons mentioned above. Maybe you haven't earned money (yet) from your writing, or haven't earned as much as you thought you should. Maybe you've been told you're wasting your time. Maybe you feel guilty for investing so much effort into something that (so far) has few visible rewards.

If you're wondering whether you should keep going, whether your writing matters, or whether you should give it up and pursue something "more worthwhile," I'm here to tell you that you are the only one who can decide to continue writing, whatever the outcome may be. The good news is, you've come to the right book. Through these pages, I'm going to take you on a journey where you'll learn ways to seriously tackle the main question that every writer faces: Does my writing matter?

This is, perhaps, one of the most important questions you'll need to ponder during your lifetime. It's a big one for any writer, and it deserves serious reflection. After all, this is your future we're talking about, so you must give it the serious consideration it deserves.

I know how you feel. You're wondering if you should continue to commit boatloads of time to this craft you love—and perhaps risk beating your head against a wall as you try to market your work—all while not knowing if it will bring you frustration, unhappiness, or perhaps (dare you dream it?) success.

Come, let's find out.

A Note to the Reader

Once upon a time, there was a writer who doubted herself. She had been writing for a few years, but had experienced only modest levels of success. One fine summer day while walking along the river, she looked up at the sky and asked the clouds, "Does my writing matter? Should I keep doing this?"

A hawk happened to fly by just at that time. It looked down on the writer and said, "Are you kidding? Of course you should! You're talented and committed and your stories move people. Don't ever think of quitting again!"

I'd love to assure you that this prophetic hawk is still out there flying around and all you have to do is look up and ask about your own future as a writer. Unfortunately, I can't recommend you go hawk hunting to resolve any questions you have about your writing career. What I can offer is the breadth of my experience wrestling with these questions along with my track record of advising other writers who are doing the same. No matter what stage of your career you're in right now, I'm willing to bet that you've had similar periods of doubt about whether what you were doing really mattered in the end.

Our time is valuable. With each passing year we are more keenly aware of the need to be sure we're using it wisely. No one wants to come to the end of life and feel like it was wasted on empty pursuits or lofty dreams that could never come true. Yet today we have so many choices as to how we might spend our time that it's become increasingly difficult to determine which are the "right" ones. We hope the seeds we're sewing today will bear fruit tomorrow, but when it comes to writing, it's difficult to know for sure.

All Writers Doubt Themselves Now and Then

I'm assuming you've been spending some time (and most likely, a lot of it) on the solitary pursuit of a writing dream only you can define, with no guarantee that time will be deemed well spent, at least in terms of tangible outside rewards. This time encompasses not only the writing itself, but also the hours striving to improve your skills and create more satisfying works while simultaneously building your author platform and getting your stories into readers' hands.

Every now and then, you step back to examine your progress. You may have accomplishments to be proud of, but disappointments, setbacks, and roadblocks too that appeared along the way. You may look at the rewards you've received so far and wondered if they were worth the effort. It's times like these when you may imagine another endeavor that would come with more tangible rewards or a bigger payday with fewer rides on the emotional roller coaster.

Every writer grapples with these questions at some point, even those who sell millions of copies of their books. If you're regularly at the top of the sales charts, though, it's easier to decide that your writing matters. In the absence of such reinforcement, the question is left totally up to you to answer, and that's not an easy task. That's why I'm here—to help you wrestle with it and dissect this intangible, but important, aspect of being a writer.

It took me a long time to decide if my writing mattered. I repeatedly questioned myself, recommitted to writing, and then questioned myself yet again, enduring a tortuous back and forth I couldn't escape. I've also met and worked with other writers who have faced these same demons. We've all heard them. They're the ones who whisper horrible words of doubt like *you're wasting your time* and *no one cares about your stories* and *you could be doing something more worthwhile with your life*.

If you're nodding because this sounds familiar to you, that's good news. I wrote this book specifically for you.

What This Book Will Do For You

Part I is devoted to examining why we writers are filled with self-doubt. Trust me: it's not just you. Writers of every genre, background, skill level, and experience go through dark periods when they doubt themselves. Most engage in self-blame, certain it's their lack of talent, marketing savvy, or even their personalities holding them back from the success they dream about. It's common to feel this way, certain that an unknown flaw stands between us and the great writers we hope to become.

I'll explain why we look to others for assurances of our writing ability or that we should even write at all, and why our own desire to write doesn't always seem like enough. We aren't living in a vacuum. The prevailing attitudes around us paired with the messages we receive every day have a powerful effect on the way we think and how we judge ourselves against our peers and even against our own standards. Understanding how our world influences our thought processes, particularly when it comes to how we judge ourselves as writers, will help you more easily navigate this dichotomy between your own desires and what the world expects of you.

Part II asks you to take a step back and reflect on the ways writing benefits you in your life, regardless of whether or not you receive any outside rewards. This pause will allow us to take a heartfelt look at the unique gifts writing has to give when we grieve, suffer from illness, or care for others needing help. We'll examine the ways writing helps us to escape from the world, release our secrets, boost brainpower, and discover the truth. I'll ask you to take the time to examine how writing affects your emotions, mood, and even your physical health, and to consider the benefits you get from your writing that you've never thought about before.

Part III gets down to asking you to seriously consider what your life would be *without* writing, and ultimately, to decide whether or not to keep going. Making this momentous decision will bring you not only inner peace but a more focused drive toward your goals, as it did for me. I believe that the process outlined here will get you there faster, saving you years of indecision, pain, and struggle.

The writer who has decided to *be a writer* no matter what the outcome is a happy, contented writer. Of course, you'll still feel discouraged and frustrated at times and even have periods of doubt. But take it from me as a fellow traveler on this road—wrestling with the question of whether your writing matters is a worthwhile endeavor. After you make this important life choice as to which direction to go, there'll be no stopping you.

Why Writers Doubt Themselves

". . . [T]he haunting Demon never leaves you, that Demon being the knowledge of your own terrible limitations, your hopeless inadequacy, the impossibility of ever getting it right . . ."

~William Goldman

ONE

Decide To Be a Writer

PERHAPS ONE OF the most torturous questions in a writer's life is, "Should I be doing this?" Learning how to write well is difficult enough without adding the pain of indecision. Yet that's what most of us endure—and for some of us, it can last for years.

For my first full decade of writing stories, I questioned whether I was wasting my time. There was no outward indication that I should be a writer. Teachers had praised my writing in the past, but no one had ever told me I should consider "being" a writer. I had started writing stories on a whim, feeling a strong urge to do so after graduating from college. But despite garnering some early publications and landing a full-time writing job, I still wondered if I had the talent to be a novelist . . . or if I was wasting my time.

Part of my indecision stemmed from failing to get a publishing contract early on. Another part of it was rooted in my own self-doubt about any talent I possessed. The feedback I received on submissions to editors, magazines, and contests didn't always help either, since some of it was positive and some, negative.

Like many writers, I went back and forth for years, sometimes thinking I could do this and other times thinking I would never reach my goals and that my writing didn't matter anyway. In the middle of it all was indecision—a difficult state of mind you may be experiencing right now.

How Indecision Can Be Painful for a Writer

Writing while remaining unsure about whether you should be writing is like riding a bicycle while dragging a 100-pound block of lead. The weight of indecision not only interferes with the act of writing. It's also the source of a never-ending supply of chronic stress and psychological suffering.

When you're not sure if you're a real writer, every writing session is tainted with insecurity, guilt, and tentativeness. You're not sure if writing is the best use of your time. Before every session, you wonder about doing something more useful. Maybe you tend to other duties first because you're not earning anything from writing, so how important can it be? Perhaps even if you do write, you may feel guilty for wasting time you could have been doing something more rewarding like enjoying the afternoon with your partner, children, or even your dog.

The urge to write, coupled with this sort of guilt, results in a lasting state of stress and pain. The internal push and pull it creates can affect you for years and hold you back from reaching your full potential, as many now-successful writers can confirm.

How Indecision Hurts You Artistically and Personally

Imagine you're driving down a road and aren't sure it's the right one. You started out thinking you were going the right way, but now things are looking a little strange. You see dead trees, a barren landscape, and a worn bridge. So you stop the car, get out, and look around. It's quiet. Eerily quiet. Not even a bird's call disturbs the silence. You get back into your car and think. You review your actions over the past thirty minutes, double-checking the map. You turned where you were supposed to, then got onto this road, which you thought was the right one.

You put the car in gear and drive forward again, more slowly this time. You keep your eyes peeled for any sign that may indicate you're going the wrong way. You stop and get out again, then get back in and drive a little farther. After a time, you turn around and retrace your steps, then decide you were on the right road after all. So you turn around again, only to end up confused a little while later. You're getting nowhere fast.

Now, imagine what you'd think if you were able to observe yourself in this confused state. You certainly would not see a confident individual getting to their destination. Instead, you would see yourself moving tentatively, proceeding slowly before backtracking and then moving forward again, scanning the sides of the road, getting out and looking, pausing, thinking, trying again, unable to confidently decide on a direction, with the result being very little progress made toward your destination.

This is the very same process that occurs when you, as a writer, suffer from indecision. You start and stop. You write for a while, but when faced with critical feedback, succumb to self-doubt and stop writing and submitting your work. Eventually, the writing calls you back. You go forward tentatively, unsure of what you're doing. Your self-doubt bleeds onto the page, visible to any editor or beta reader. When you regain the courage to show your work, you receive feedback that makes it clear that your writing lacks confidence. Discouraged, you stop again.

Struggling to decide which road to take on a trip is much the same as struggling to decide if you're a writer. To solve the problem, you must sense your purpose and feel that it is tied up in your desire to write. Focusing on that inner knowing is the key to finding the steadfast commitment you need to fulfill your potential as a writer.

Through my decade of indecision, a dim fog clouded my focus much of the time. But I was sure it would clear once some outward sign strongly indicated that I was supposed to be a writer. While I waited for a force outside myself to make this decision for me, that fog blurred my vision of the future and clouded my awareness in the present. I teetered between being a writer and not being a writer, or from being a creative, artistic writer of both fiction and nonfiction to being only a copywriter for skincare products and heart disease brochures.

It was a confusing time, but it's a process that all writers must navigate as we work to uncover the clarity we desire. Until then, we often feel like we're riding an unending roller coaster. Fortunately, you can save yourself years of this type of confusion if you realize that what you need is already deep within you.

The American Idol Syndrome

I'm a big fan of NBC's *The Voice,* and I've seen *American Idol* a time or two. Though I love watching the singers grow and compete, it's painful to witness the indecision projected by just about every contestant in their interviews before they go on stage for the initial audition. This is when you hear all sorts of variations on the theme of, "If I'm chosen, then I'll finally know I should be doing this." And by inference, "If I'm not, I probably should quit and go back to my day job."

Many of these contestants are brilliantly talented. Others have been performing for years or have cut albums. Some are involved in hometown community music groups or are singing sensations on YouTube. My point is that you'd think they would have already decided to sing no matter what, but that's rarely true. Just about every one of them, regardless of their experience level, says something like, "If I can make it here, then I'll prove I should be doing this." Or, "If I get a chair to turn, I can finally leave my job." Or, "If I can get to LA, I'll feel like I belong in this business."

They're no different than writers who leave the final decision up to others. And it doesn't stop there. At their core, these artists don't just desire to hear someone say, "Yes, you're a great singer and you should keep singing." What they're really hoping is that these shows will offer a way for them to sing as an *occupation*—that their television exposure will get them recognized as singers with a hefty paycheck to go with it. They want this not only for the glitz and glamour (though that's tempting enough), but for the final clarity they seek. If they produce an album, make money, and garner many fans, their ambivalence is put to rest: They *are* singers, they're supposed to be singing for a living, and there is no more indecision about it.

For us writers, it's not television we crave (unless we're dreaming of being on late-night talk shows). Rather, we want the same sort of validation from traditional publishers, contests, and readers. Perhaps you're trying for that contract with one of the Big 5 or another publisher that pays big advances (which, in truth, are nearly non-existent these days) and facilitates wide distribution. Should a major publisher say yes to your manuscript, then questioning yourself as a writer would be over. It would finally be clear that you were meant to write and you wouldn't need to worry about it anymore. What a relief.

Or maybe you're looking for confirmation from readers and bestseller lists. If your book becomes a *New York Times* or *USA Today* bestseller, then you have that badge of honor attached to your work and can finally believe you're a good writer and should keep writing.

When we look outward to society to make this type of decision for us or to put an end to our indecision, we are shortchanging ourselves. How many times have you heard a writer say, "I'll give it five years, and if I haven't made it by then, I'll do something else"? That's a writer who's without confidence and being hampered by indecision. A writer who's hoping someone else will figure out their future. A writer who's wishing for the publishing version of a chair turn.

Indecision May Exist in the Shadows

You may be thinking, *This doesn't sound like me at all. I've decided to write. I'm writing regularly. I get in so many words per day. I have so many completed manuscripts. This doesn't apply to me.*

To be sure about that, here's a little quiz I'd like you to take. Answer each of the following questions by choosing only one of the two available answers. If more than one seems applicable, choose the one that's true *most* of the time. Be brutally honest with yourself. Pretending to feel differently than you truly feel will rob you of the insights the quiz could provide.

1. When I receive a rejection, bad review, or any sort of criticism, I:
a) Consider any benefit I may gather from it, then move on.
b) Question whether I should be writing.

2. When family and friends complain about the time I spend writing, I:
a) Let it roll off my back and perhaps schedule other time to spend with them.
b) Feel guilty for choosing to write instead of spending time with them.

3. When I see another writer succeed in a big way, I:
a) Wish them well, but I don't feel it has anything to do with me.
b) Feel envious while thinking I should be further along by now.

4. When I finish another story, I feel:
a) A sense of peace and accomplishment.
b) Like I haven't done as well as I'd hoped.

5. When I think about the money I've earned from my writing, I feel:
a) Content with where I am.
b) Frustrated I haven't earned more.

6. I sometimes think that maybe I should be doing something else with my time and talents.
a) True
b) False

7. If you asked me if I'd still be writing twenty years from now, I'd say:
a) Yes.

b) I'm not sure.

8. Most of my friends and/or family don't really know about my writing.
a) True
b) False

9. I long for the day when a publisher, an award, or a best-seller's standing will elevate my writer's status.
a) It would be nice, but I'm okay either way.
b) Yes, something like this would make me feel more confident.

10. I often feel like I'm not sure if this is the right path for me.
a) True
b) False

Now total your A and B answers separately. If you have three or more B answers, you're still stuck in indecision. Also, be aware that even if you marked only one or two Bs, you may be struggling with indecision on some level. Only the person who marked ten A answers has truly decided to write no matter what.

Conquering Indecision

If you're struggling with any degree of indecision, it's okay. Most writers do. That's why I wrote this book! If you're feeling pretty sure about your identity as a writer, that's good, but read on just in case. Listed below are other signs you might not be aware of that indicate you're not as decided as you thought.

How to Tell if You're a Writer Who Hasn't Yet "Made the Decision"

For at least half of my writing career, I thought I was serious about it. But in truth, I was like that partner in a relationship with one foot out the door. I spent years writing and doing all the things a writer does, but I still hadn't fully committed. You might be in the same boat right now. How can you tell? Check for signs like these:

- When things don't go well, you consider giving up writing.
- You often question whether you should be writing.
- You make agreements with yourself like, "I'll be a writer when I get published," or "I'll be a writer when my book becomes a bestseller," or "I'll be a writer when [fill in the blank]."
- You allow outside events to sway your commitment to writing.
- You spend your writing life in a constant state of questioning: "Am I really a writer? Do I have the talent? Should I be doing this?"
- You're like a leaf in the wind, sometimes feeling like your writing career is secure and other times feeling like you're wasting your time.

Now, it's extremely common for writers to feel all these things and more. Who are we to think we can succeed at this? And who wouldn't doubt their ability after a rejection, bad reviews, poor sales, or any of the other things we go through that shake our confidence?

But here's the thing: If you're still in a place where you're questioning whether you are a writer, should be a writer, have the talent to be a writer, and so on, that means one thing: You haven't yet *decided* to be a writer.

As you can see, it's similar to being in a relationship. When a person gets married, it is expected that they have committed exclusively to their partner, no matter what. That's why they said their vows. There is no more questioning. No more debating the issue. It's decided.

The same thing occurs when a writer decides, "I'm a writer. Like it or not. No matter what you think. I'm writing because I've decided writing is important to me, and there's no more debate about it."

Warning: You can't achieve this sort of commitment simply by making a statement like, "I'm a writer." Truly deciding to be a writer involves much more than simply voicing what you *hope* is the truth. It's a process you must go through to emerge on the other side convinced of the rightness of your decision.

Indeed, you can do all the things a writer does to pursue a writing career and still be an undecided writer. The shift to "decided" doesn't show up on the outside as much as it does on the inside. It takes root over time and with each obstacle you overcome. Whenever you experience a setback and decide to keep writing, you cement writing's role in your life.

Your Ultimate Decision About Writing Comes from Your Previous Decisions

Scientific evidence supports the idea that the more you choose writing, the closer you'll get to your ultimate decision to be a writer, no matter what. Researchers from the University of Melbourne found via brain scans that every time participants chose something—like writing—they built a preference for that choice.

Over time, choice after choice, something changes until you realize that yes, you've made the ultimate decision. You look up and say, "You know what? I don't give a rat's ass anymore what anyone says, what the agents or publishers think, or how many of my efforts fail. I'm a writer. And that's that."

Three Things That Happen Once You Decide You're a Writer

Once you truly decide that you're a writer and feel that decision settle solidly inside you, a few things happen.

First, you're less likely to be blown about by outside opinions, no matter whose opinions they may be. Sure, a rejection or a poor review still hurts, but it doesn't throw you back into that painful state of indecision. It doesn't make you question whether you should keep writing. Instead, you grieve, then pick yourself back up and write some more.

Second, you gain freedom. You care less about what others think or how your book may do in front of agents, editors, or the market. This may even extend to feeling more freedom on the page. After all, you are the writer, and it's up to you how the story unfolds. So it makes sense to be braver in your approach. It becomes easier to bring your entire self to the task and give it your all, to take a few risks and push the boundaries.

Third, you achieve a definitiveness of purpose that shows in every part of your writing career. And that definitiveness—surprisingly enough—may bring you a level of success you haven't experienced before.

There is Power in Making Decisions

Oprah Winfrey is quoted as saying, "Nothing happens until you decide. Make a decision and watch your life move forward."

Deciding that you're a writer is one of the most important decisions you'll ever make. You can't force it. You can't rush it. When it does come, take it from me: Your life as a writer will get even better after that.

I Know I'm a Writer Because . . .

I've interviewed hundreds of writers on my websites. Many of them stand out in my memory for one reason or another, but one, in particular, comes to mind now. I can't remember the exact words she wrote, but I remember the moment I read them.

I was getting the piece ready to post on my website. I read about the writer's emotional struggle with self-doubt and the ups and downs of her life as a writer. She said something about wanting to continue because she enjoyed the act of writing, then followed it with this bombshell: "I'd drop it in a heartbeat if I knew I should be doing something else."

Those words stopped me cold when I read them. I felt so badly for this poor writer. I could see that she hadn't yet made the decision and was wishing desperately for someone to make it for her. I wanted to reach out and tell her that she would never find her answer that way and that, even if she did by way of winning an award or having a book on a bestseller's list, it would still leave her with slivers of doubt. The only way she could ever find real peace in knowing she was a writer was to make the decision herself.

Society's expectations, coupled with our own craving for external rewards, give us a fake sense that only those writers who have achieved fame are worthwhile and, therefore, only the well-known and celebrated are truly fulfilling their purpose. The rest of us—no matter how gifted—are silly to continue devoting time and effort to this writing thing as long as we're doing it without outside acclaim.

But it doesn't matter what others think. You are either a writer or you are not. You decide, not the outside world.

It's not an easy decision to make. I'll continue to explore the issue in the following pages. For now, get out your journal and answer one question:

I know that deep down I'm a writer because:

A)
B)
C)

TWO

How to Put the Question of Talent to Rest

WRITERS OFTEN ASK ME, "What if I'm not talented enough?"

I understand this question because it haunted me for years. We ask it because we believe (mistakenly) that talent alone is what separates successful writers from unsuccessful or not-as-successful ones. Wrapped up in that belief is another that says we can't *learn* to be better writers. We may discover how to polish things up a bit, but we'll never go from being individuals who write to being "real" writers—let alone great, successful writers— if we don't have a certain level of talent.

As you discovered when overcoming indecision, there's no outside force that can tell you if you have the talent to write. Nevertheless, for most writers, it's a never-ending quest to find out. We mistakenly think that once we get someone—a teacher, mentor, editor, and/or agent—to confirm our talent, we'll gain the clarity we need to be able to make "the decision" and move forward as legitimate writers.

Talent versus Ability versus Desire

Talent is defined as having a natural aptitude or skill for something, though I prefer Angela Duckworth's way of describing it. She's a professor from the University of Pennsylvania and the author of the *New York Times* bestseller *Grit: The Power of Passion and Perseverance.* Professor Duckworth has done extensive research on what it takes to succeed, and she describes talent like this:

"When I say 'talent,' I mean specifically the rate at which a person improves in skill. So, if you're a talented basketball player, you improve very quickly when compared to less talented players with equivalent practice and opportunity." Duckworth goes on to say that she believes there are differences in talent level and that people are not equally talented. I agree. We can all see this in our children. One may have natural musical ability, while another is a natural athlete. That doesn't mean the athlete can't learn to play the piano or the musician can't enjoy playing sports. What it does mean is that each will excel at different levels, depending on their natural abilities.

Writing is no different. Most writers know they have an aptitude for writing if it comes easily to them or if they have a knack for stringing words together. They write not because of outside pressure, but as a response to an inner desire.

Is that feeling indicative of talent or ability? That's where it gets confusing. Just because we *like* to write doesn't mean we're naturally good at it. After all, you can enjoy playing baseball and not be able to hit or catch a ball to save yourself.

That said, it's entirely possible to enjoy writing and not have the talent to become a great writer. This can leave a writer in a state of indecision for years. That's why many of us search for confirmation from others whom we wish would please tell us whether we have writing talent or are simply one of the many mediocre writers with limited prospects for lasting success.

The Talent Trap

Despite our great desire for clarity in this area, there are three problems with trying to define talent in any individual:

1. Talent is not the most important factor for writing success.

2. It *is* possible to learn to be a better writer.
3. No one is qualified to judge writing talent.

1. Talent is Not the Most Important Factor for Writing Success

Angela Duckworth discovered that it wasn't talent, test scores, intelligence, or top-ranking schools that produced successful graduates, but rather a combination of passion and perseverance—or what she calls "grit."

The child who continues to practice the piano will eventually surpass the equally gifted child who divides her time between the piano and the saxophone because it's more about the totality of effort, passion, and perseverance than it is about talent. When one is gritty, one perseveres no matter the obstacles. One gets back up after falling, recovers after failures, and keeps marching toward one's goals. One *desires* success, and it is that desire that fuels the effort needed to achieve success.

"As much as talent counts," Duckworth wrote in *Grit,* "effort counts twice."

I've found this to be true in my French horn studio. I've taught French horn lessons for over twenty-five years, so I've had the opportunity to work with a lot of very bright students. Out of a total of about 100, five that I know of have gone on to become extremely accomplished adult players and continue to perform in musical groups today. Only one individual in that group is what I would call exceptionally gifted. The others all had talent, of course, but so did most of my students. In fact, it was extremely unusual to find a student without at least some talent. Instead, it was more common for them all to exhibit musicality in one form or another. One might have a great sense of rhythm, another could hear where the pitches should be, and another was quick to pick up the rules of music theory. What separated the top-performing students from the rest was exactly what Duckworth also found: hard work and determination. The exceptional students practiced regularly, pushed themselves to do better, and disciplined themselves to continue to develop their skills even when they didn't feel like it. Underlying all that hard work was one other extremely important factor for success: desire.

Every one of my students who went on to become lifelong top performers *desired* it early on. They strived to play well and stand out in their musical groups. They loved music and felt a deep sense of accomplishment when they performed a passage well or took home a musical award. They competed for musical scholarships to help them pay for college and practiced to impress their teachers with their progress.

Music and writing are very similar pursuits. Each requires practice, devotion, and a desire to consistently improve. Talent is not the most important factor—far from it. If you focus on your desire to get better, in all probability you will.

2. It Is Possible to Learn to Be a Better Writer

There's a myth in the writing world that great writers are not made, but born. Of course, we can all point to examples of child prodigies and masters blessed with natural writing gifts. These people are the literary greats, the classic poets, the popular genre stars, and the esoteric geniuses.

When we do this, we shortchange the tens of thousands of excellent writers out there—some of whom are "successful" by society's terms, and some of whom are not. To prove this to yourself, head down to the library or review the latest releases at the bookstore. I know that not a year goes by when I don't read a new work by an author who blows me away. Good writers keep popping up, so surely that means it can be learned.

Story doctor David Farland agrees: "As an instructor, I find that if I describe a problem well, suggest solutions, then give the writer an exercise, the writer can almost always gain new writing skills pretty easily. In fact, about one-third of the time, I'm amazed at how well the writers do. They almost seem to grow magically."

There is no shortage of writing classes filling high school and college curriculums. There are also community classes, online courses, and convention workshops that teach writing. In any given year, there are thousands of writing classes across the country. This means people are learning to hone their writing skills all the time, and they're succeeding. Plot, characterization, pacing, setting, dialogue—all of these techniques and more are taught.

That's the great thing about being a writer: The learning never stops.

3. No One is Qualified to Judge Writing Talent

It is possible to accept that you can learn more about writing but remain unsure about your level of talent. You may hunger for that little bit of praise from an established writer, editor, or agent because you don't feel qualified to properly judge your own gifts. So you look to others to do it for you, which is why an editor's positive comments can send you to the moon or a rejection can leave you down in the dumps for weeks. Don't fall into the trap of thinking that if you get it from a good authority that you *do* have talent, you can put that question to rest and finally get to work. It's always a boost to get affirmation of your writing talent. But what if the authority instead tells you that writing isn't for you?

I've heard plenty of stories from writers who went through this sort of soul-crushing experience. They were told by a teacher, editor, or even a spouse that their work wasn't "good enough" and that they would be smart to spend their time on something else. But why is this low opinion to be believed, either?

The truth is that *no one* is qualified to evaluate your talent. Sure, an experienced editor can help you improve your story. A book doctor can assist you in overcoming plot problems or pacing issues. A good writer's group can point out inconsistencies in your characterizations. But no one—absolutely no one—is qualified to evaluate whether you have enough talent to be a good writer.

On the off chance you don't believe me, let me ask you this: Who do you imagine would or should have the power to evaluate or judge whether you have enough writing talent, whatever "enough" is? What being would you allow to wield that sort of power over you? Certainly not your writing teacher, editor, spouse, or parent, or even a reviewer who didn't like your book. There's no one in my life to whom I'd be willing to surrender that power. I hope you feel the same.

It wasn't always this way for me, though. I, too, once thought a bestselling author would know whether I had talent. Then I went through a workshop where the bestselling author-teacher summarily shot down my story and quickly moved on to the next. The message to me was clear: I didn't have the talent to warrant more of her time. I was crushed—and certain my writing life was over. By a stroke of luck, though, I had mailed that same story to an editor a few weeks *before* the workshop. When I returned home, I found a request for the full manuscript. I promptly sent it and soon after was offered a publishing contract.

Of course, as writers, we must realize that everyone is entitled to their opinions and that our work will be judged subjectively by a variety of people. Those people have every right to say what they think of a story in a review or critique, but not to judge whether you have writing talent. Even the work of great writers doesn't appeal to everyone, and we must be prepared to face criticism. But never should we believe that such criticism is somehow indicative of our level of talent. A person can be qualified to evaluate your story, but no one is qualified—no matter how many accolades they have, how many millions of books they've sold, how much they say they "know" you, or how much authority they have over you—to determine whether you have the talent to succeed.

Steven Pressfield, the author of the great book, *The War of Art*, wrote a blog post titled "Nobody Knows Nothing." I highly suggest you read it. (You'll find the link in the references list at the back of the book.) In this blog post, he writes, "Make every effort to break the habit of listening to other people's opinion of your work. Not one person in a hundred is qualified to give feedback to a writer, including me."

If you have the desire, love to write, and feel like your life would not be complete without writing, don't jeopardize that drive by giving someone else the power to defeat it. Choose for yourself whether you will write. What truly matters is the strength of your determination to succeed and your willingness to do the work to attain the skills you'll need to do so.

No One Can Evaluate Talent, but They Can Evaluate Skill

Now that you know that talent cannot be evaluated, don't make the mistake of thinking that you don't need feedback on your work.

There's a difference between evaluating talent and skill, and it is this: Even though you may have talent as a writer, you might not have developed your storytelling skills enough to be a published writer. While no one is qualified to evaluate your level of talent, editors, agents, book doctors, and others can evaluate your skills.

Again, imagine a child with musical talent. That child can pick out tunes on the piano without any assistance, but she has no skills in reading music or understanding hand and finger positions. And so her progress remains limited. Regardless of how talented she is, she will remain unskilled until she gets some instruction and achieves a higher level of mastery of the instrument.

Skills, unlike talent, can be learned, practiced, honed, improved, and mastered. They are measurable. Talent is not. As a writer, your focus should be on developing your skills. You can work on your ability to write good dialogue, for instance, or create taut plotlines. With practice and instruction, you can deepen your characterizations, enliven your action scenes, and paint more colorful pictures of your settings. The more you do this, the better your chances of living up to the potential your talent suggests.

"The best way to acquire a skill set within any discipline is to learn from those who have mastered it," writer and coach Shulem Deen tells us, "and with writing, too, the best way to master the craft, is to learn from others. What makes a reader care? What makes sentences come alive? What kinds of words have the strongest impact? What gives a piece of writing order and cohesion? Those who've mastered the craft have the wisdom to help us answer those questions. This means that writing can most definitely be taught. The question is only: are we willing to learn?"

Never allow the issue of talent to stop you from seeking feedback on your work. Focus on the skills you need to develop, and the question of talent will take care of itself.

Early in my writing career, when I was struggling to get a publishing contract, I hired an editor to help me, and it was one of the best decisions I ever made. She praised those areas of my writing that showed promise and gently pointed out the areas that needed more work. Her instruction provided clear guidance on what I needed to focus on specifically, and my writing improved as a result. What's more, during the whole time I was learning, practicing, and evaluating, I never once worried about or questioned whether I had enough talent.

Remember the writers I told you about at the beginning of this chapter who asked if they were talented enough? They would have been better off asking how they could improve their writing. That's a question that can be answered, and one that will garner truly helpful advice.

Stephen King once said, "Talent is cheaper than table salt. What separates the talented individual from the successful one is a lot of hard work." Amen to that.

∼

Put the Question of Talent to Rest

Put the question of talent to rest by completing this quiz:

1. Do you love to read?
   ____Y ____N

2. Do you dream about being a great writer someday?
   ____Y ____N

3. Do you often doubt your ability as a writer?
   ____Y ____N

4. Do you love new office supplies like pens, paper, and planners?
   ____Y ____N

5. Do you find it difficult to express yourself verbally, but easy to do so through the written word?
   ____Y ____N

6. Do you frequently make up stories in your head about people you see in random places?
   ____Y ____N

7. Do you find time to write, no matter what?

____ Y ____ N

8. Do you frequently find yourself lost in thought, often about a story?
____ Y ____ N

9. Do you love the sound of a perfect sentence?
____ Y ____ N

10. Do you lose track of time when you're writing?
____ Y ____ N

11. Do you frequently jot down story ideas on pieces of paper, on your smartphone, or in other places?
____ Y ____ N

12. Do you love talking about books and other stories?
____ Y ____ N

13. Do you easily get wrapped up in characters' lives, whether those characters are on the page or screen?
____ Y ____ N

14. Is about half your life spent inside your head?
____ Y ____ N

15. Does writing bring you joy?
____ Y ____ N

Total yes and no answers: ____ Yes ____ No

If you had more than seven yeses, you have the talent you need to be a writer. (Yay!) There's your answer. Feel better now?

If you scored fewer than seven, don't give up based on one questionnaire. It was just for fun anyway. The questions do apply to writers. But in truth, the results have absolutely nothing to do with writing talent.

Instead, let's continue to explore the question of how much your writing matters—and, therefore, whether you should continue doing it. Talent, as we've learned, really has nothing to do with future success and shouldn't factor into your decision. But making money, which I cover in the next chapter, just might.

THREE

The Alluring Traps of Money and Fame

AT THE TIME I was writing this book, the most recent Authors Guild survey of more than 5,000 writers revealed that, between 2009 and 2017, author earnings declined to a historic low: a median of $6,080 per year. Earnings from book income alone fell even more, declining 21 percent to $3,100 in 2017 from $3,900 in 2013 and just over 50 percent from 2009's median book earnings of $6,250.

There are several reasons for this, but it points to the overwhelming fact that most writers don't make a full-time living by writing books. How this affects our culture and industry are topics for a different discussion, but I draw your attention to it here to make you question more seriously if you are tying your identity as a writer to whether you are making money from it.

I've heard writers express concern that they don't feel like "real" writers because they make little to no money doing it. This may be because we live in a culture where making money is important—*really* important. A national survey found that, when asked what they valued most in life, more Americans answered "money" than "friendship" or "religion."

Why Money Is So Important

It's not just friendship and God that play second fiddle to money in today's world. Vacation time does, too. A survey by finance recruitment firm Accounting Principles found that, given the choice between an extra week of vacation and a 5 percent increase in salary, nearly 80 percent of respondents chose the higher salary. (For comparison's sake, one week equals about 2 percent of one's salary, so a 5 percent increase is equal to two-and-a-half weeks off.)

It's easy to see why someone might make this choice when struggling to make ends meet. But the researchers discovered that even people making high incomes preferred the extra money.

Current research also shows that three out of four American college students consider it "very important" or "essential" to become "very well off financially." That's nearly double the numbers from 1970. In 2018, the "Making It in America" survey by US manufacturer ThermoSoft asked 2,000 Americans this question: "If you haven't yet 'made it,' what's missing?" About two-thirds of respondents (or 67 percent) said "income." When asked what salary would signal success, the average was $150,000 per year, which is more than double the national median income.

You've probably noticed this particular focus on income yourself when visiting with family, friends, or colleagues. People are more likely these days to point out how much a particular athlete earns in a year or what a celebrity is paid to star in a movie. The old joke about children growing up and being lucky enough to find doctors and lawyers to marry is still in style, as these are professions that frequently come with high salaries. When a neighbor drives home in a fancy car, it's still common to see raised eyebrows among the other neighbors, who soon get together to gossip about where so-and-so got the money for that.

We writers do it, too. We dream of substantial advances and massive worldwide book sales that result in six-figure royalties. We make note of those writers who get movie deals, believing they come with a fat payday along with the big boost in exposure. We also buy book after book by the "bestselling" authors, believing that books that sell well—thereby making their authors a lot of money—are better than those that don't.

But believing doesn't make it true. A revealing article by Lynn Neary that was published on NPR's website pointed out that, in the United Kingdom, the Booker Prize-winning titles often have disappointing sales—certainly compared to bestsellers. For example, Tom McCarthy's *Satin Island*, one of six finalists for the prize, had sold only 3,600 copies at the time it was listed. *The Green Road* by Irish author Anne Enright had sold only 9,000. Compare that to the 100,000 or more sold by more big-name authors.

Award-winning or not, it's the proven bestselling authors who get the biggest marketing push from publishers. As a result, major advertising money translates into the public being familiar with their names and, therefore, deeming them to be among the best. They become our models, and we dream of joining their ranks.

Yet, according to a Written Word Media survey, only 11 percent of authors earned $100,000 or more from their writing in a year. A Digital Book World survey in 2014 revealed far lower numbers: 0.7 percent of self-published writers, 1.3 percent of traditionally published, and 5.7 percent of hybrid writers (both traditionally and self-published) reported making more than $100,000 a year from their writing.

Nevertheless, writers who aren't making what they deem to be "enough" from their writing often question what they're doing, particularly if they write and publish for years with only modest results. Despite this very real data, the idea persists that we must make money—and a good amount of it—or we're simply not good enough.

If Not Money, Then Fame

When a writer thinks of money, it's not only about paying the bills or supporting a comfortable lifestyle. Money to a writer also means readers—and, dare we say it, fans.

You know this is true. In today's world, it's more about being "seen" than ever before. A study done on a group of children between ten and twelve years old found that the desire for fame—solely for the sake of being famous—was the most popular future goal. It overshadowed the desire for financial success, achievement, and finding a sense of community. In a 2017 survey of millennials conducted by social talent sharing startup Clapit, more than a quarter of respondents said they would quit their jobs in exchange for fame, and *one in twelve would completely detach themselves from their family to become famous.*

The Need to Become Famous

When Dara Greenwood and colleagues looked into *why* people desired fame, they found three main reasons:

1. To be seen or valued
2. To enjoy a high-status lifestyle
3. To use fame to help others, or to make friends and family proud of them

"To be seen" was the main reason people sought fame. This natural need is a part of human psychology. When it's not fulfilled in daily life, it becomes a driving desire that propels us to seek it beyond those boundaries.

Wanting to learn more about this need to be seen, scientists from the MIT Sloan School of Management and the University of Chicago Booth School of Business conducted an experiment where they paid participants to complete a simple, repetitive task. Each person was given a piece of paper printed with a sequence of letters. They had to find ten examples of where two consecutive letters appeared. Once they finished, they had to hand in the sheet to the experimenter to receive payment. There was a catch, however: The payment was lowered with each sheet completed, so the participants received less money each time. The question was how long the participants would keep working as the payments diminished.

The scientists put an additional spin on the experiment. The participants were broken up into three groups:

1. **Group One (Acknowledged):** When the participant handed in the sheet, the experimenter looked up at the participant ("saw" them), quickly reviewed the answers, and filed the sheet away before granting payment.
2. **Group Two (Ignored):** When the participant handed in the sheet, the experimenter took it (without looking at the participant) and filed it without reviewing it, then granted payment.
3. **Group Three (Shredded):** When the participant handed in the sheet, the experimenter looked at it (but did not look at the participant) and immediately shredded it before granting payment.

Results showed that those in the first group—the ones who were "seen"—kept working significantly longer than those in the other two groups, completing over one-third more sheets of paper. There was no difference between the completion rates for the Ignored and Shredded groups.

This experiment shows the pure power of acknowledgment—of having our work seen or recognized, no matter how briefly. It motivates us and encourages us to keep going. It also demonstrates that when our work is ignored, it has much the same effect as if the work was shredded into tiny little pieces.

It's clear, then, that everyone has some form of this desire to be seen. For writers, however, the need can become a driving one to where, if it's not fulfilled to our expectations, we can grow discouraged to the point of giving up.

How to Become a Famous Writer

If you Google "how to become a famous writer," you will find hundreds of articles with titles like, "How to Become a Famous Writer: 12 Steps," "The Secret to Becoming a Famous Writer," "23 Tips from Famous Writers for New and Emerging Authors," and "These 7

Writers Got Famous While Keeping Their Day Jobs." You can quickly see that this is a popular topic among aspiring writers.

The desire to be famous most likely stems from the human need to be seen and feel a sense of belonging. Scientists believe that, in the past, this desire provided an evolutionary advantage, as those who were approved of and liked gained the protection of the group and were more likely to survive. Those who were not were often shunned and isolated and were more likely to die off. As a result, we have a population that seeks and desires acceptance and approval.

Not only is it normal to seek acceptance within our social groups at work and home, during leisure-time activities, at church, and in our communities, few would argue that this desire for attention and fame has evolved and today is even easier to attain thanks to the Internet.

Internet Fame Becomes Accessible to the Masses

"Certainly wanting to be the next big celebrity isn't anything new," writes Daryl Nelson for *Consumer Affairs*, "as each generation had its portion of wannabe rock, movie and TV stars, but since the rise of the Internet, along with its ability to give the average person an immediate audience, the kid who spent his time gazing at the ceiling dreaming of stardom from his bed, has leapt off the mattress and headed to the nearest computer to show the world what he can do artistically."

Indeed, psychologists frequently comment about how the Internet and social media have created a "look-at-me" culture, with a large segment of the population desiring fame, not because of any particular accomplishment, but simply to feel accepted.

A poll of 1,000 sixteen-year-olds from the United Kingdom found that more than half didn't want a career—they just wanted to be famous. Similarly, a Harris Poll involving over 3,000 children between the ages of eight and twelve found that being a YouTube star was a more sought-after profession than being an astronaut among kids both in the United States and the United Kingdom. And a 2007 Pew survey found that "getting rich and famous" was a high priority for eighteen- to twenty-five-year-olds.

The Loneliness Factor

A driving need for fame can result from being rejected early in life. It may also arise simply because of our natural desire to forge relationships. Loneliness is an epidemic in today's culture, and many people search online for ways to help fill that space in their lives.

In a recent survey of over 10,000 Americans by health insurance company Cigna, more than three in five reported feeling lonely, a 13 percent increase over the previous year. Interestingly, the investigators reported that social media use was tied to loneliness as well, with 73 percent of very heavy social media users considered lonely as compared with 52 percent of light users.

The Unhealthy Desire for Fame and Attention

Combine loneliness with access to the Internet and social media, throw in a dash of our normal need to be seen—which, for some, may be exacerbated by life experiences—and you have what can be an unhealthy desire for fame and attention. Writers can fall victim to this sort of desire, and many do.

I've attended several writers' conferences and sat through boring conversations with writers who cared only about puffing themselves up. Their desperation for approval was obvious and not fun to witness (it's often quite sad); and as irritating as it can be for others, it's usually worse for them because the behavior is isolating, which is the opposite effect of what they hoped to achieve. Even those who have similar longings for attention and approval but have enough self-control to keep it under their hats unknowingly increase their risk for rejection. These writers often come across as bottled up and self-involved, making any attempt to show interest in others seem blatantly inauthentic.

This display of desperate need is seen on social media, too. We've all been exposed to the countless Twitter tweets and Facebook posts from writers promoting themselves ad nauseam. Sure, all writers need to promote their work now and then, but thousands post nothing else but images and text about themselves and their books, again achieving the exact opposite of what they're hoping for. They're ignored rather than celebrated, shunned rather than accepted.

Another reason writers fall into this bottomless pit of self-promotion is because they think that's what marketing themselves is all about.

"I Have to Market Myself"

When I got my first publishing contract, like many other writers, I was encouraged to open a few social media accounts and get a regular blog going. Being a very private and reserved person, this made me uncomfortable. But hey, the publisher said I needed to do it, and I was eager to have my book do well. So off I went.

My efforts met with lackluster results because, like many authors, I had no idea what I was doing. Authors today are simply told that marketing their books is mostly up to them. For some, it comes as a total shock. Others expect it but are still woefully unprepared as to how to go about it. After all, it takes years of dedicated practice to become a publishable writer. It's a difficult prospect, to say the least, to find the additional time and energy to educate oneself on marketing and self-promotion—skills that, at their essence, are dramatically opposed to the act of creating.

For most writers, this is extremely challenging and often soul-crushing. Still, many suck it up and jump into the fray. Like me, they open social media accounts and start blogging because that's what they are told to do.

Unfortunately, without a basic understanding of the principles of marketing, these attempts create lackluster results, often because the writers use these tools as "look-at-me" portals with unfiltered posts as to the goings-on in their own lives, including personal stories, images, and (of course) everything and anything to do with their work. When these attempts don't receive the longed-for recognition, writers tend to blame themselves—and down the path of discouragement they go.

The Danger of the "Platform"

Writers indeed need to be "known" to sell books. Publishers and agents seek writers who already have a platform or a ready-made audience. Unfortunately, those of us who aren't already somewhat established on the market often end up eternally stuck in this vicious world of "all about me" when trying to "put themselves out there" to win an audience and achieve that elusive dream of fame.

Most writers work hard, and many are extremely talented. Yet unlike reality shows would lead us to believe, not every talented individual receives the recognition they have earned or may deserve. It doesn't matter how many "buy my book" tweets a writer posts or how many free chapters they give away. There are simply too many talented people out there, many of whom know how to market themselves effectively or—perhaps more often—have the money to pay others to do it for them.

This makes the publishing industry a difficult one in which to survive for the creative, often introspective writer. As I said earlier, the writer who has what it takes to create a publishable book often spends oodles of precious time and energy trying to market their books in the best way they know how, only to be disappointed by the results. This heartbreaking and destructive path leaves countless talented individuals limping along from one disappointing project to the next—and for some, it results in foregoing a writing career altogether.

Author Sheridan Voysey wrote about an experience that brought this concept home. In 2005, when he was a brand new author, his publishers had arranged for him to be interviewed at a book fair. When the time came, he walked out on stage, expecting a big crowd, and looked out to see only four people—and two of them were his publishers.

He later wrote, "After the interview I stopped to sign the one book sold then made a hasty exit, where I found myself walking against a stream of people heading to hear the celebrity about to speak next door. I got in my car and sat for a while . . . feeling very *insignificant*. . . . [T]hat day I saw the problems of measuring your self-worth by popularity. Hard to get and easily lost, when we base our significance on it, despair is soon to follow."

Indeed, the problem with pursuing attention and fame is typically that there is never *enough* of it. Writers who receive ten reviews want twenty. Those who receive 100 will lament not getting 1,000.

> "The fundamental truth about the fame motive is that it's never satisfied and people have to live with it all their lives," Orville Gilbert Brim, author of *Look at Me! The Fame Motive from Childhood to Death*, told author Daryl Nelson in *Consumer Affairs*. "However hard they try to become famous, they'll fail to get what they're after."

Why "Becoming a Famous Writer" Is Such a Difficult Goal

I'm not saying you can never become a famous writer. But I do want to help you see how difficult it truly is to save yourself from such blame if you never reach this elusive goal.

The Realities of the Book Market

These are the cold, hard facts about the book business:

- Each year, more books are published than the year before. In 2017, self-publishing grew at a rate of more than 28 percent—an 8 percent increase over 2016—according to ISBN agency Bowker. The total number of self-published books grew from about 786,000 to over one million for the first time in *one* year. And that's not counting traditionally published books. This means that a market already stiff with competition gets even more competitive by the year.
- Books must compete with many other forms of entertainment for people's attention, and it's only getting harder. According to a 2018 Pew Research Center survey, nearly a quarter of American adults hadn't read a single book in the past year. A recent American Times Use Survey

conducted by the Bureau of Labor Statistics found that Americans over the age of fifteen spend about 0.28 hours, or about 16.8 minutes, reading for personal interest each day. That's down from twenty-one minutes in 2007.

This shouldn't stop you from seeking approval and fame as a writer. There's nothing wrong with dreaming big. What often happens, though, is that when we writers don't achieve our lofty goals, we end up feeling empty, discouraged, and disheartened. At times like these, we ask ourselves, "Does my writing matter?"

As if those feelings aren't bad enough, they can get worse when cousin Eddy, work colleague Elaine, or neighbor Judy looks disbelieving when you assert yourself as a writer. Unfortunately, this can wrongly reinforce the feeling that what matters isn't the quality of the work itself, but how well the work—and the author—are known. Indeed, you can blame it on our culture, which every day emphasizes that only those who are famous are valued.

Writers *Need* Readers

Most of us will eventually set aside the "big money" dream of a $100,000 per year writing income in favor of more modest success. Once we realize the challenge and understand it's an uphill battle that can be approached with a more realistic view, we gain the ability to celebrate smaller successes as the achievements they are.

It would be nice if we could do something similar with the desire for fame—or, more accurately, the desire *to be seen*. We could just write and *not care* about whether we become known. Unfortunately, such an approach would result in most writers feeling unhappy and unfulfilled.

The sticking point is that the writer-reader relationship is *critical* for a writer's development. Without it, a writer not only misses this critical interaction but also lacks the type of feedback readership can provide—the feedback that compels an author to improve with each succeeding work.

A writer needs this necessary back-and-forth—publish the book, get audience feedback, work on the next book, publish it, get audience feedback, start on the next book, etc.—so they don't feel discouraged and invisible. It takes positive emotions inspired by reader feedback to nurture a prosperous career.

But what happens when, after a few lackluster book launches, a writer settles for being satisfied with writing works that are rarely read? This is a difficult prospect. Who among us, even the most creative, are willing to devote hours and hours to something few will acknowledge?

The worst-case scenario is that the writer gives up, believing that a lack of readership is a commentary on the quality of their work rather than a failed marketing campaign or a young author platform. This mistaken assumption misleads the writer into living an uninspired and unfulfilled life, believing that their gut instincts to write were all wrong.

Somewhere in between these two extremes is where most of us live, battling against our discouraged feelings while returning again and again to the blank page, running ourselves ragged trying to build up a readership however we can.

What I am telling you is that writers who enjoy fulfilling, rewarding careers—even if they don't sell a lot of books—are the ones who find ways to develop healthy relationships with their readers. Rather than seeking money or fame, they've learned that it's more important to seek *connection*.

The Motivation to Affect Other People Drives Creativity

In a 2013 study, researchers Marie J. C. Forgeard and Anne C. Mecklenburg from the University of Pennsylvania looked closely at what motivates creative people to produce their work. Past research had shown that the main motivator of creative behavior was the intrinsic interest in and enjoyment of that behavior. In other words, writers become writers because they enjoy writing.

Sure, some people start writing for other reasons—to boost a business, for example, or in the hopes of achieving that notoriety we've been talking about. But those who stick with it and have a desire to write regardless of whether they achieve success are driven by internal factors. That's only part of the story, though.

"Recent studies examining the nature of motivational processes driving creativity have however highlighted the importance of a second dimension of motivation," wrote Forgeard and Mecklenburg. Indeed, in addition to that intrinsic motivation to create, "creative work may also be driven by its effect on the creator and *on other people* [emphasis mine]."

Most research on creativity has positioned it as a solitary and self-centered endeavor where the sole intended beneficiary *is* the creator. Yet this viewpoint fails to acknowledge the crucial part played by others in the creative process.

Not only are writers influenced by readers, but writers also hope that readers will, in turn, be influenced. "Indeed, creative products are generally meant to be experienced both by the creator and by others," Forgeard and Mecklenburg wrote, "and creators therefore may hold important motivational goals for what they want their products to achieve."

Author Holly Robinson wrote about this subject in the *Huffington Post*. She talked about attending a book-signing event where she didn't think she'd sell many books. "As I lugged my box of books up the icy driveway that night," she wrote, "part of me was longing to be at home, sacked out on the couch and reading or watching TV." She hadn't started marketing her book *Sleeping Tigers* yet, so she wasn't expecting much. She was surprised, therefore, when several women approached her table excited to get a copy: "One of the women explained that there were two book clubs attending the event, and the members had all agreed to read my novel. Then she leaned forward and confided, 'I've had breast cancer, too. That's why I want to read your book.'"

Holly went on to visit with several of her readers. "The stories that many of the women told me as they stopped by my table lingered with me for a long time. We talked about breast cancer and motherhood, travel and books, husbands and jewelry, among other things." She ended up selling twelve books that night. But though that was nice, it wasn't what mattered to her. "Afterward, as I toted my empty cardboard box back to the car, I was reminded again why being a writer is the most spectacular pursuit in the world: as you share your own stories with others, readers share their lives with you in return."

Happy Writers Connect with and Inspire Readers

It's fascinating to read the results of the studies that have delved into this concept. They show that creators are often inspired by a desire to help others—or simply to connect with them. Polman and Emich (2011), for example, found that creating for the benefit of another led to more original works than creating for oneself. A result of this research led Forgeard and Mecklenburg to come up with a two-dimensional framework of motivation in creativity where one must take both into account as well as consider the interaction between them:

1. The creator's motivation to do the work
2. The intended beneficiaries of that work

This framework, as creators are already aware, shows that our work is not only influenced by the world but that we also hope to influence it in return. Our ability to get feedback on our finished works and how they affected others helps influence how we approach our future work.

Forgeard and Mecklenburg explain this in more detail by suggesting that we are driven by four possible combinations of four different motivations:

The creator's motivation:

1. Growth (intrinsic):
a. The creator's desire to grow in their work—to become a better writer

b. The desire for that feeling of "flow"
c. The sense of attaining meaning from writing

2. Gain (extrinsic):
a. External rewards from the work
b. Examples such as financial compensation and recognition

The beneficiaries:

3. Guidance (focused on the creative process itself):
a. Educating or teaching others through the process
b. Meeting the expectations of others (mentors, teachers)

4. Giving (focused on the outcomes of the process—the work or final product)
a. Evoking pleasure (a fun read)
b. Helping others acquire knowledge
c. Solving problems affecting others
d. Making others feel emotionally validated
e. Challenging others with complex works
f. Communicating with others; connecting

Interestingly, the Growth/Giving combination was the most commonly seen among creators. Motivated by both self- and other-oriented concerns, the creator creates a product and sends it out into the world to influence others. The others then review and offer feedback, which, in turn, influences the creator.

I might have never gotten into writing nonfiction books had it not been for reader feedback. As I started building my platform and hearing from my blog readers, I took notice of where writers were struggling and the areas in which they needed help. It was this interaction alone that inspired me to write *Overwhelmed Writer Rescue, Writer Get Noticed!,* and this book as well. My relationship with readers has broadened my entire writing career in ways I could have never foreseen—and in ways that have been incredibly rewarding and inspiring.

This is exactly the type of cause and effect Forgeard and Mecklenburg mentioned in their study: "The dynamic nature of this process may also explain developmental changes in creators' motivations. For example, an author who initially writes for personal pleasure may speak with fans and learn that her work helps them through difficult experiences. In subsequent work, this information may translate into new or strengthened prosocial motivation for writing, which may then prompt the author to experience greater self-oriented benefits as well."

The Loop

The takeaway for us as writers is that our work is at least partially motivated by the desire to positively contribute to others' lives. This completes a loop, and if part of the loop is missing—readers, for example—a writer is left feeling incomplete at best, and a failure at worst.

"Of course, there is a part of every writer that longs to be on the *New York Times* bestseller list," Holly Robinson wrote in her *Huffington Post* article. "We would all love to make enough money from writing to put our kids through college, or even put a dent in the grocery bill. More important than that, though, is our longing to connect with readers on an emotional level."

So it makes sense that, without that connection, we're left grasping at straws, posting a million "buy my book" tweets, and checking the sales figures for the fifth time in one day to see if anyone—please, anyone!—decided to read our book.

"For most writers," Robinson wrote, "every book takes months, even years, to write. We don't know how, or even if, that book will ever be published in the end, but something compels us to keep going. That 'something' is the reader."

How we find readers without blindly chasing after money and fame is a subject for an entire book (check out *Writer Get Noticed!*), but the crucial first step is to thoroughly understand what the real goal is. Dig deep enough, and you'll find that it's not lots of Facebook likes you really want or even sales in the thousands (though we'd all enjoy that). The truth is that a writer desires to connect with readers. Achieve this goal, and you complete that loop we've been talking about.

Forget Money and Fame—Focus on Connection

When you're seriously considering whether your writing matters, I urge you to keep money and fame out of your analysis. I hope that, in reading this chapter, you've come to better understand that the key to happiness and fulfillment as a writer is making connections with your readers. When you keep your focus on helping *them*, that takes the focus off yourself and allows you to approach building a platform with a sense of service to others. Do this in earnest, and readers will respond by making that all-important connection. Continue this process, and your audience will grow.

What Benefits Do Readers Get from Your Work?

Which of the following potential benefits does your writing provide most to readers? Even if you think that more than one applies, for this exercise I want you to choose only the one that matches your work *best*. If you don't see one that fits, feel free to come up with one of your own:

- Educating or teaching others

- Providing others with pleasure or fun
- Solving problems affecting others
- Making others feel emotionally validated or valued
- Making others think in ways they haven't before
- Communicating with others; connecting
- Entertaining others
- Making others laugh
- Giving others a thrill
- Other: _____

Now, think about how you might use the benefit you've chosen to best market your work. How might you target your giveaways, blogs, social media posts, in-person presentations, and more, using this goal as your guide? If you want to educate others, for example, how would you do that through your author platform?

Brainstorm possible approaches, and try them to see what feedback you get. Then use that feedback to adjust and fine-tune your approach for even better results. (For more detailed information on how to do this, see my other book, *Writer Get Noticed!*, which has specific exercises in developing a successful author platform.)

FOUR

Writing as Part of Your Life's Purpose

SINCE YOU'RE READING this book, it's likely that your writing holds special significance for you and that you're not just doing it for fun or as a lark. You may even hope you're not being foolish in thinking that writing is part of the reason you're here on Earth.

I started my professional life as a teacher. I was naturally good at it, and it felt meaningful to me. Yet I still wondered if my sole purpose in life was to teach. Deep down, I had this nagging feeling that, although I enjoyed teaching and found it rewarding, it wasn't something to which I could devote myself completely. My mind and heart desired something more.

When I experienced a calling to write, I was still in my early twenties. I wasn't sure where it came from, only that I suddenly felt compelled to try my hand at storytelling. It so happened that I had the time and freedom to experiment before plunging back into the workforce full-time, so I took full advantage of it and gave writing a try.

Within three years, I had a full-time writing job and had turned my entire career around. I still wasn't sure, though, whether my "purpose" in life was to write—a question I've since heard from many other writers, and maybe you feel the same. Even though we are drawn to write or "called" to write, we still doubt whether writing is part of what we were put on Earth to do. We think that it is and we'd like it to be, but we worry that these thoughts are reflective of a big ego or self-deluded fantasy.

It's common to wonder whether we are "good enough" to justify giving writing such importance in our lives. Self-doubt leads to questions such as, "Should I be spending all this time on this if writing is not what I was meant to do? Am I only fooling myself?" We undermine our confidence; and with every rejection or less-than-enthusiastic review, we think that perhaps we've been mistaken about writing being part of our purpose and should go back to the drawing board.

Why Purpose Is Important

Purpose is important for one reason: Once we find a purpose in life and commit to it, we feel good about doing it regardless of whether we make money or gain recognition. Therefore, I propose that finding purpose is the perfect solution to the writer's modern-day conundrum. If your purpose is to write, then you won't be so worried about whether you're selling books, making money, or becoming famous. It won't matter as much because you'll be secure in knowing you're doing what you were designed to do with your life.

Unfortunately, there is no purpose fairy flying around, assigning purposes as decreed by some all-powerful king. Determining whether writing is part of your life's purpose is *your* job—something you alone must decide. It should be as simple as determining whether writing is a worthwhile endeavor. But in today's society, it's more complicated because purpose has become intertwined with occupation—often to the detriment of both.

Finding Your Purpose

When you search "what is your purpose?" online, you'll receive thousands of links to sites offering answers. Most suggest purpose can be found in one or more of the following three areas:

1. Vocation (meaningful, satisfying work)
2. Family and friends
3. Spirituality and religion

To find our true purpose is to find out who we are and where we belong. But most of all, purpose is about figuring out what we should do with our lives, with the implication being that it should be something important.

I'm sure you'd agree with this sentiment. We want our lives to matter, so we need to believe we're doing something meaningful at least part of the time. To this I say, writing surely qualifies! But not so fast. Here's where it gets sticky. What defines meaningful? Few would argue that writing a Pulitzer Prize-winning novel means the writer dedicated their life in a meaningful way. Writing a moving memoir or reaching a bestseller list often carries the same weight. Achievements such as these, we think, are proof that the writer did indeed find their purpose in writing and, as such, lived a meaningful life.

But when you take a closer look, it's the same old message on replay. When you sell a lot of books (i.e., get rich) or gain widespread recognition (i.e., become famous) via an award or large audience, then what you did mattered. It was important. Once again, the message is that when writing makes you rich, famous, or both, it must have been that your life's purpose was to write.

But what if you don't reach any of these pinnacles of success? That's where it gets more complicated. What if you simply write and perhaps publish, but then sell only a few hundred books? What if your only award is an honorable mention in a contest or a handful of five-star reviews? What if you release your book and few people notice? Does that mean you must question whether all the time you spent writing was warranted or meaningful?

These are very difficult questions to answer without a closer look into the meaning of purpose.

Why Having a Purpose is Beneficial

Having a purpose is indeed a good thing, but we need to delve deeper to see why. Here are some of the reasons why defining your purpose is so beneficial.

1. Defining Your Purpose Helps You Focus

Once you decide what your purpose is, it's easier to focus on the activities that support that purpose. You gain clarity and make better choices about how to spend your time. Setting goals becomes a simpler task and working to achieve them part of your routine. Suddenly, your path is clear and you no longer feel lost or unsure. You simply put one foot in front of the other and go on down the road.

Think back to what it was like when you were in high school and not sure of what you wanted to do with your life after graduation. Maybe you had some idea, but when you started college, you found you weren't on the right path or your chosen area of study wasn't as fulfilling as you thought it would be. Or perhaps you got your degree, but your resulting profession didn't live up to your expectations.

We all go through periods when we're just not sure where to go or what to do next. Once you discover your purpose, that sort of questioning and feeling of insecurity disappears, and finally you can focus on what's most important.

2. Knowing Your Purpose Opens the Door to Opportunity

When you clearly define what your purpose is and determine how you want to pursue it, you open yourself up to new opportunities. Suddenly, people appear who can help you, or new positions become available that you may have never noticed before.

Gaining clarity of purpose focuses your intentions, which, in turn, helps you to make the choices that create the right opportunities. This is the time when coincidences and synchronicities are most likely to occur—when things tend to fall in place the way you need them to.

3. Defining Your Purpose Makes Life Easier

Once you define your purpose, you free up your brain to enjoy the process of pursuing it. No longer are you trapped in indecision or questioning. No more does your brain have to wrestle with whether you should be focused on this option or that one. Instead, there is a clear line between you and your destination, and you can put all your focus on accomplishing your goals.

It doesn't matter what your purpose is. It is the act of defining it that helps rid you of any guilt or negative feelings associated with how you spend your time. This allows your creative self to thrive.

4. Purpose Gives Your Life Direction

Scientists from George Mason University published research in 2009 that illustrated how purpose— defined as "a cognitive process that defines life goals and provides personal meaning"—leads to an overall healthier and longer life. People with purpose are more likely to experience better mental and physical health, increased life satisfaction, and a longer life expectancy.

The scientists explained that having a purpose not only helps you organize your life goals but also gives you motivation for acting in healthy ways that will help you reach those goals. They compared purpose to a compass—that thing that gives your life direction.

"Living in accord with one's purpose," they wrote, "offers that person a self-sustaining source of meaning through goal pursuit and goal attainment."

5. Knowing Your Purpose Helps When You're Weathering the Down Times

When you pursue a goal with a sense of purpose, obstacles morph from roadblocks to exciting challenges. A writer who pens a novel to make money is likely to be shaken to the core after receiving ten rejections and might give up entirely, figuring there's an easier way to reach their goal (which there likely is).

On the other hand, a writer who pens a novel with the knowledge that their life purpose is in writing will be equally shaken after rejections but is more likely to recover and try again. A strong purpose brings resiliency.

"Purpose motivates people to persist rather than quit in the face of difficult situations," wrote McKnight and Kashdan, adding that it also "enhances rebound capacity" and that people with purpose "will be less prone to illness and report fewer symptoms even when ill."

6. Having a Purpose Protects Your Mental Health

If you have struggled to determine what your purpose is, you understand how it takes its toll mentally and emotionally. Scientists know that the opposite—clearly defining your purpose and living according to that decision—can protect one's mental health.

In a 2013 study, researchers reported that individuals with social anxiety disorder experienced substantial boosts in well-being on the days they were making efforts or experienced progress toward their life purpose. This suggests that having a purpose not only protects mental health but may also help improve symptoms of mental illness.

In 2012, researchers questioned over 400 men who had just enlisted in the Navy. Those with a higher sense of meaning in life were less likely to suffer symptoms of depression. Researchers also noted that higher meaning in life correlated with better physical and mental health.

7. Having a Purpose May Help You Live Longer

Having a purpose may even stave off mortality. In a study involving over 6,000 people, those who could articulate the meaning and purpose in their lives died later than those who saw their lives as aimless. In fact, those who lived with purpose were 15 percent less likely to die than their aimless peers.

In another study, scientists observed over 9,000 people with an average age of sixty-five for about eight-and-a-half years, during which time they had the participants answer questionnaires about their "eudemonic well-being." This relates to a person's belief that their life is worthwhile as well as to their sense of purpose. The scientists then divided the participants into four groups based on their answers, ranking them from the highest level of well-being to the lowest. Those in the lowest well-being category—those without a strong sense of purpose—were more likely to die during the study period than those in the highest category.

"Once all the other factors had been taken into account," noted the University College London in a press release, "people with the highest wellbeing were 30 [percent] less likely to die over the study period, living on average two years longer than those in the lowest wellbeing group."

The False Hope of Living on Purpose = Rich

As you can see from the research, having a purpose in life—or multiple purposes—benefits us in many ways: mentally, emotionally, physically, and spiritually. You may have also noticed that there was no "live on purpose, get rich" subheading listed above. That's because one action doesn't necessarily lead to the other, even though we've been led to believe that it does.

Just take a look at the following headlines.

> Do What You Love, and the Money Will Follow!
> Four Reasons Why Living Your Purpose Can Make You Rich
> Want Wealth? You Need to Find Your Purpose
> The Formula to Get Rich Doing What You Love
> Turn Your Passion Into Profits!

They go on and on. Indeed, our culture has become saturated with these types of messages. We're told that if we discover our purpose and then fulfill it or "live it," riches will follow. Plus, it will feel effortless because, after all, we're doing what we love!

Choose a Job You Love?

Choose a job you love, and you'll never work a day in your life. ~ Confucius

So-called gurus selling courses and books that promise to help you get rich by living your purpose love to parrot this quote. It neatly sums up what they are selling: the promise to fix what's wrong in your life by helping you discover what your purpose is (as if it's as easy as plugging numbers into a secret formula), then guiding you toward finding the business or career that allows you to live this purpose, with the result being you wallowing in bags of money while living your dream.

There's no denying that this is an attractive idea, which is why so many people are peddling it. But in most cases, it only leads to disappointment. I'm not saying it's impossible to make money doing what you enjoy (far from it, actually), but getting rich is on another level entirely. It requires a different sort of lifestyle—one that, for many writers, is difficult to sustain.

The fantasy for a writer is to simply write and watch the money come in, but let's take a closer look at that. You love to write, so you write. The money, however, as most writers will attest, doesn't just fall in your lap after you publish a story. For most of us, to make money writing, we must market our work, and that requires a different skill set. This is the polar opposite of the writer's skill set or personality. It requires the writer to become a salesperson and hawk their beloved prose as merchandise. The writer must morph into someone who can create marketing plans, analyze return on investment, track sales related to publicity, stack up opportunities to get their work in front of new audiences, and generally do everything a publicist might do but a writer isn't programmed to do.

Still, if you're serious about writing to make money, it's something you can learn to do. Some writers enjoy the adventure. They dive in, eager to learn about marketing and book promotion. They take the appropriate courses, attend conferences, and implement their plans to see how they turn out. They love getting together with other entrepreneurs who are working to make more money from their books; and if they stick with it, they often succeed. Of course, as with learning any business, this takes a big investment in terms of money and time—time not spent writing, that is.

But we know many writers aren't wired this way. Talk to them about marketing plans, Amazon ads, sales tracking programs, analyzing financials, and the like, and their eyes roll back into their heads. This wasn't part of the "do what you love" program they signed up for.

I've seen it again and again in the writers who come up to me at conferences and workshops, or who email me, all with the same basic lament: "I'm trying to market my work and make money, but it's not going very well and I'm discouraged." Of course, coping with discouragement is part of life and definitely part of the writing journey. But what scares me is seeing the light dimming in these writers' eyes. They all started out excited about writing, but by the time they come to me, that excitement has dwindled. The fire is going out.

This is when I worry that they will give up writing altogether. It pains me to hear, "If I can't make money at it, then I probably shouldn't be doing it." This is often what happens to the thought process, even for writers who believe that writing is part of their life purpose, when making money becomes a goal. This mode of thinking reflects today's culture where money, it seems, infiltrates everything.

There was a time in my life when I decided to get serious about making more money with my work, mainly my books. I invested a couple of years doing all the right things: building my newsletter, writing guest posts, doing speaking engagements around the country, planning book launches, implementing giveaways, conducting book blog tours, giving interviews, going on podcasts, reaching out for reviews, and more. Then I'd obsessively track my sales numbers. When the numbers went up, I'd celebrate. When they didn't move, I'd get discouraged. In the end, it wasn't a sustainable lifestyle for me. That marketing took far too much time. Supporting myself on a freelance writer's salary didn't allow me to invest in a publicist or marketing agency, and doing it all myself was emotionally draining. The bottom line was that it robbed me of the time to do the work I loved, which was writing.

What's more—and as if it could get any worse—I was focusing more on marketing my work than actually *creating* the work. I was getting far too wrapped up in my abilities and achievements as a marketer rather than as a writer, which, in hindsight, I realized was ridiculous. I certainly didn't have the background, experience, education, or inherent skills to ever become a star marketer.

My focus on making money also interfered with my feelings about my work. I started to view it in a negative light based on sales and profit, which led to a twisted mindset: *If the books aren't selling thousands of copies, they must not be very good.* This defeatist thinking wasn't even true, as these books had won numerous awards.

This self-questioning about whether I was wasting time on any new project—because it was highly probable that it would fail to make big bucks—paralyzed me creatively. I began imagining all the marketing activities needed to sell this next book and felt my energy drain right out of me. I began to ask myself, "Why bother?"

The whole experience was what I call "soul-sucking." You may have experienced something similar. You pour your heart and soul into writing a book, period. When you finish it, there's a sense of accomplishment, a glow of light that shines within you. *I did it*, you think. *I did it, and it's good.* But then you start focusing on sales, money, marketing, and getting people's attention, and it's like holding your heart and soul outside of your body and asking people to set it on fire.

I'm reminded of a quote from the movie *Hope Floats*, in which Sandra Bullock is Birdee Pruitt, a young mother devastated by her husband's recent affair, and Harry Connick Jr. is Justin, her former boyfriend who spends his free time restoring old homes. During one tender scene between them, Justin shows Birdee a house he's restoring and she's astounded by its beauty. She asks him why he simply paints houses as his day job when he's a true architect who's capable of creating something so breathtaking. He could do so much more, she says, with the implication being, *Live your purpose and get rich!* But Justin doesn't buy it and says, "You find something that you love, and then you twist it, and you torture it, try and find a way to make money at it. You spend a lifetime doing that. At the end, you can't find a trace of what you started out lovin'. What did you start out lovin'?"

I imagine many writers—maybe even you—feel this way at times, particularly after a long period of trying to "get rich doing what you love." It pulls us away from what matters: the writing.

I've been lucky in that I've found a way to market my work that is now much more rewarding and enjoyable. I talk about this in *Writer Get Noticed!*, but the point here is that your purpose in life doesn't have to make you a lot of money, and thinking it does often leads to angst and discouragement.

Purpose Has Nothing to Do with Money

An interesting study published in 2016 in the *Journal of Research in Personality* seems, at first glance, to support the notion that if you do what you love, you'll automatically enjoy financial wealth. The *Inc.* article that discussed this study used this for a headline: "Scientists Say Finding Your Purpose Could be the Key to Financial Success." It suggests that finding one's purpose and turning it into a compatible occupation means ending up wealthy and happy.

Once again, when we dig a little deeper, we find it's more complicated than it appears. For the study, Patrick L. Hill and his colleagues examined data from about 5,000 people who were interviewed twice: once between 1995 and 1996, and again between 2004 and 2006. The average follow-up period was about nine years. The scientists focused on the participants' sense of purpose in life, their income, life satisfaction, net worth, education, and personality traits. Those who were determined to have a high sense of purpose were those who reacted to these types of questions in the following ways:

- They strongly agreed with this statement: "Some people wander aimlessly through life, but I am not one of them."

- They strongly disagreed with this statement: "I live life one day at a time and don't really think about the future."
- They strongly disagreed with this statement: "I sometimes feel as if I've done all there is to do in life."

"[I]ndividuals who reported a higher sense of purpose in life tended both to have higher household income and net worth initially," the researchers wrote, "as well as greater increases on these outcomes over the following decade."

But—and here's where the message that having a purpose can make you rich has gotten muddled—it wasn't about aligning one's occupation with purpose. The people who scored high on feeling a sense of purpose weren't necessarily "doing what they loved to get rich." Instead, their sense of purpose—whatever it was—positively affected their mindset and outlook in such a way that they were more likely to experience greater levels of success in life.

Having a purpose, the researchers noted, is linked to "greater agency and engagement in life," as well as "a number of positive health outcomes. As such, the value of purpose for financial success may result from the greater capability and propensity for purposeful individuals to pursue long-term goals, which in turn promotes the accrual of assets."

In other words, it's more about *how* having a purpose affects your overall approach to life—how it contributes to your ability to maintain good mental health, weather the downtimes, focus on goals, and find new opportunities. You may feel that your purpose in life is to raise strong, healthy children who give back to the world. With that purpose in mind, you go forth to make that a reality, and that mindset affects everything you do, including your job (whatever that job may be). If you work consistently toward your goals, you're more likely to achieve them.

The same thing can happen if you believe your purpose is to write. With that purpose in mind, you do what you need to do to give yourself the time and freedom to write, and that purpose fuels you. It gives you focus, energy, and drive, and that affects every part of your life—as long as you don't mess up and focus on making money instead.

Finding Purpose to Create Meaning in Your Life

When my parents were growing up, a job was about making money, period. Back then, you found your purpose in other ways, often through your family, community, and spiritual endeavors. Today, we're urged to not only find a job and make money, but to also love every moment we spend on that job. If we don't, we're told that something is wrong, as obviously we haven't yet lined up our purpose with our occupation.

There's nothing wrong with trying to make money by writing. But if, somewhere along the way, you find it's damaging your love for writing, it's time to step back and reevaluate. In truth, living your purpose has nothing to do with getting rich. It's about finding a reason to get up each morning. When you have a sense of purpose, it guides your decisions, behavior, and goals. It gives your life direction. Perhaps most importantly, it gives your life *meaning*—and that, certainly more than money and fame, is what most of us are interested in finding.

Which brings us to the inevitable question: What does your writing mean to you?

What Does Your Writing Mean to You?

Answering this question brings you smack up against your ego. You have to face the fact that you may have—just a little bit—hoped your writing would bring you notoriety, respect, and admiration. You may have hoped it would give you a way out of your boring job. You may have wanted it to win you a place among those other writers you've long admired.

Answering this question also forces you to face the possibility that none of these outcomes may be possible, because if they did happen—if you received the admiration you desired, for example—you wouldn't be struggling with this question of what your writing means, right? We struggle when our dreams *don't* come true or when they haven't yet come true. We struggle when the ego doesn't get what it wants. We struggle when we come up against the pure difficulty of the journey, so we question our ability to keep going.

It is precisely when we reach this crossroads that we must seriously examine our motivations and answer this question: What does writing mean to me? In a way, the conditions that cause you to wrestle with the answer are gifts, because they force you to face this issue of making meaning with your writing. Until you do that, you're standing on shaky ground, for the writer who knows exactly what writing means is the writer who perseveres, no matter what.

Eric Maisel, a psychologist, creativity coach, and author of multiple books on creativity, has said that creative people are unique when it comes to needing to make meaning with their work:

> "[C]reative people are people who stand in relation to life in a certain way—they see themselves as active meaning-makers rather than as passive folks with no stake in the world and no inner potential to realize. This orientation makes meaning a certain kind of problem for them—if, in their own estimation, they aren't making sufficient meaning, they get down."

Maisel helps us understand that making meaning is important not only to our writing but also to our overall well-being. It's a similar concept to having a purpose. Having a purpose or making meaning makes living life worthwhile. What we have to do is find what is important to us as human beings and not base that importance on whether those things produce money or fame.

Your writing will mean precisely what you decide it will mean in your life. No matter the outside success. No matter the sales. No matter the accolades. It will mean what you decide it will mean, period. Is it part of your purpose in life, or not?

How to Determine If Writing is Part of Your Life's Purpose

As this chapter has pointed out, it is not an easy process to determine the answer to this question. I invite you to reflect on the following points and perhaps journal about them to get a better idea of where your heart is when it comes to your purpose and how writing may or may not fit into it.

1. Realize that you alone must determine meaning.

Meaning does not exist until you make it exist for you. This is not something that is "out there." The answer is inside you. You have this gift, this desire to write; and you must determine what it means in your life and what purpose it will serve.

2. Reinvent your definition of success.

Whereas before you may have defined success as becoming a best-selling author or signing a publishing contract with one of the top five publishers in the nation, it may now be more realistic and rewarding to simply finish your novel, self-publish your book to your satisfaction, or carve out more time in your busy life for writing.

3. Accept yourself as you are.

Wholeheartedly accept that you are a creative person who needs to make meaning with your work. Realize that this is just as important to your health and well-being as eating a nutritious diet and exercising regularly. You cannot change or overlook this inherent part of yourself, so embrace it.

4. Find meaning in other activities.

As a creative individual who craves meaning, you may need to find additional ways to make it. Writing may be enough, or it might not.

Some people also find meaning in relationships, standing up for a cause, being of service to others, or in successful careers. By being open to finding meaning in multiple purposes, you may come to enjoy writing even more.

5. List all of the activities you find meaningful.

Take about thirty minutes to contemplate your writing life so far. Using your computer or a notepad, record all of the writing-related experiences that were particularly meaningful to you. Perhaps it was when you gave a reading, worked with students, shared your thoughts on a blog post, connected with other writers at a conference, finished your novel, or got a scene just right. Get them all down where you can see them, review them, and relive them.

Drawing your attention to these positive life events will help you see which ones are worth repeating and which ones can help you set meaning-based goals for the future.

6. Make the most of your writing talent.

Sometimes we limit our potential by taking a narrow view of what writing encompasses. I never considered that building an author platform would open up new ways for me to find meaning with my writing. Creating blogs for writers, speaking at workshops, and writing nonfiction books has helped me fulfill that desire for meaning in ways that writing novels alone never did.

Consider how you could expand your writing activities to bring more meaning-making opportunities into your life. Pursue those that interest you even a little bit. Experiment. Don't be afraid of making mistakes. You may be surprised at how rewarding it can be to branch out into something new.

7. Use your creativity to help others.

Start by thinking of ways you can use your talent to help others.

Your answers will provide you with a direct path to creating purpose. To get you started, here are some suggestions:

- Mentor other writers, and/or support their efforts on social media or your blog.
- Write an important remembrance for your family.
- Use your writing talent to support a cause that matters to you.
- Share your experiences or expertise as a writer with local schoolchildren.
- Hold a workshop to get other writers started on their stories.

Brainstorm a list of ideas, write notes, and keep your eyes and ears open for new opportunities. When you take notice, you'll see them.

Making Writing Part of Your Life's Purpose

If you're still unsure of what writing means in your life, answering the following questions may help you decide.

- Would you still write if you were to never sell a book, reach the bestseller's list, or win a contest? If so, why?
- Think back on the feedback you've gotten from others on your writing. What is your most treasured piece of feedback? Why

and how did this one statement influence you or make such an impression on you?

• What piece of writing are you most proud of? Why? What is it about that work that makes it special?

• What do you most hope that others will get from reading your writing? If you could describe it in one word, what would it be? How about in one sentence?

FIVE

If Not Money and Fame, Then What?

I'LL NEVER FORGET the first time I was paid for a piece of writing.

It was in the mid-'90s, and I had submitted a children's story to a small print magazine. They accepted the story—my first acceptance—and sent me a check for ten dollars. I framed that check. It still sits on my desk today as proof that someone thought my writing was good enough to deserve monetary compensation, even if the amount was low.

Indeed, most writers seek this type of validation, as it confirms our writing as worthwhile. We often prefer monetary rewards because our culture best equates them with success. As we progress and become seasoned writers, it's only natural to expect the rewards will increase in value. It doesn't always work that way, though; and when the money doesn't flow as expected, we suffer not only because we're conditioned to believe these are the rewards most worth pursuing, but because their absence leaves a *gap* behind. We worked hard for the reward. If there is none, what did we do all this work for?

Fortunately, there is a satisfying answer to that question, but you have to do some reflecting to find it.

Humans Are Built to Seek Rewards

I once had a German shepherd, Morrigan, who was really good at getting rewards. If she wanted a bone, she would perform every trick she knew in the hopes of winning her prize. These included sitting, lying down, playing dead, sitting up, and shaking hands. Sometimes she'd perform one after the other in a frenzied series of movements, then look at me with her caramel-colored eyes, gauging my reaction. If I made any other motion besides handing her the bone, Morrigan would go through the whole routine again. She wanted that bone, and she did everything she knew how to do to get it. She usually succeeded.

We humans are much the same. We are conditioned throughout our lives to actively seek out rewards and act as needed to get them. Babies cry and their parents attend to their needs, such as hunger, nurturing, or a diaper change. Crying evolves into learning to behave in certain ways to gain rewards like gold stars on a chart, high grades, an allowance, praise from parents and teachers, and more.

As adults, we continue down this path of reward-seeking. We work a job for a paycheck, benefits, and a sense of security. We put in extra effort for the reward of a promotion and/or a raise. We may take on a second job to afford a house, car, or vacation. We exercise every day to maintain our health and appearance. And so it goes.

That our brains are hardwired to seek rewards is one reason why we can't seem to stop scrolling our Twitter and Facebook feeds looking for "likes." Psychologists call this the "dopamine-seeking reward loop." Every time we receive a reward, the brain releases dopamine, a neurotransmitter that makes us feel good.

Dopamine is also involved in other brain functions such as thinking, moving, and sleeping, but it's critical in producing feelings of pleasure and enjoyment. As such, it motivates us to behave in ways that will result in these feelings, even if those behaviors are bad for us. Dopamine is what motivates addicts, for example, to seek out drugs or alcohol. It compels people with weight issues to consume high-fat and high-sugar foods. It persuades smokers to light up. The release of dopamine is just too powerful to ignore. We keep wanting more . . . and more . . . and more, riding an endless loop around and around.

That's not to say it's all bad—far from it. This process also compels us to repeat positive behaviors such as engaging in a hard workout to experience heady endorphins or putting in extra hours at work for a bigger paycheck. It drives us to get out another blog post in anticipation of reader comments or to pen another chapter to get closer to writing The End. Whether we experience benefit or harm from dopamine depends on what we're doing to activate it.

The key to dopamine's power is its ability to create an emotional association with reward. Without dopamine, we may understand that we worked hard to earn a paycheck and appreciate the monetary value of that paycheck, but experience little emotion in response to it. Dopamine allows us to *feel* something, which is what motivates us to repeat the behavior.

Think about how it feels to receive a book award, for example. The award itself may be nothing more than your name listed on a website or a sticker you can place on a few copies of your book. You can't take these rewards to the bank, but the emotions they elicit make them worthwhile. When the announcer calls your name and invites you to step up in front of your peers and receive that certificate, dopamine is released in your brain—and that makes you feel wonderful.

What's interesting is that the *expectation* of receiving a reward has an even more powerful influence on our emotions and motivations than the actual reward itself. It's why just the thought of selling a lot of books, getting that publishing contract, or seeing your book on the bestseller's list is enough to motivate you to get back to work on your story. You can imagine how it will *feel* to get that reward and, oh, you want to feel that feeling. You want it a lot! So you are likely to work hard for it.

The bad news is that if the reward is less than you expected or hoped for, the dopamine signaling decreases. If your book launch is as successful as expected or even more so, you'll get the dopamine hit you were hoping for and, with it, the impetus to move on to the next goal. But if you sold fewer copies than expected, your motivation for writing could suffer, leaving you discouraged and unsure about your future.

We've all been there. When hoped-for money, fame, or even just a modicum of book sales don't happen, we can feel flooded by negative emotions from disappointment to discouragement to fatigue. You know, the emotions that trigger that dreaded question: "So why am I doing this?"

Addressing the Gap Between Work and Reward

Wherever you are in your writing career, there's no doubt you will eventually confront what I call the Gap. This is the void that occurs when the money and fame you hope for fails to materialize. You work your tail off anticipating those rewards, and when you don't receive them, you experience the Gap, the emptiness that comes in place of the reward.

The most common reaction is to find another way to fill it. You may surrender and say, "Okay, fine, I don't have to be a bestselling author. I don't have to get rich off my book sales or have thousands of fans. As long as I can just [fill in the blank], I'll be happy." The variations on this are endless. Some writers claim they'll be happy with so many books sold—pick a number. Others say they'd be happy with enough money from sales to suffice as a side income. Still others shoot for recognition with contest wins or glowing reviews.

Once you make this deal with yourself, you'll work hard again in the hopes of achieving whatever new goal you set. Around the dopamine loop you'll go again, setting yourself up to either succeed or fail, depending on what you chose.

Here's a secret: The writers who choose well at this point go on to enjoy writing for the rest of their lives. Those who are unrealistic in their expectations will continue to suffer from discouragement and indecision and may stop writing altogether.

The difference between these two groups is this:

- The writers in the first group learned their lesson and set better goals the next time around.
- The writers in the second group simply got back on the same loop.

"Better" goals have two things in common:

1. They are more likely to be within your control.
2. They are smaller and more achievable.

Let's look at each of these characteristics in more detail.

Focus on Goals That Are Within Your Control

You can do everything right—write a great book, have it professionally edited and proofread, establish a strong author platform, and run a well-thought-out marketing plan—but you can never control or predict how readers will respond. No one can. Doing the right things increases the odds that your book will sell. But know that in the end it's up to the market, and sometimes even the best books get ignored.

Experienced writers understand this. After a few turns around the block, they realize that they can't count on outside rewards, so they *focus on different goals.* Instead of shooting for money or recognition, they may focus instead on writing a book they feel intensely proud of, improve their writing skills overall, telling a story that has deep meaning for them, or making connections with a target audience of readers.

Two Types of Motivation

Intrinsic Motivation

The above goals are completely within a writer's control, and they involve what is called *intrinsic motivation,* or motivation that comes from within. When you're intrinsically motivated, you have a desire to achieve a goal for your own personal purposes. Pursuing the goal satisfies a longing within you and has nothing to do with any outside forces or influences.

A mountaineer who wants to climb Mount Everest simply because he's long desired to see the view from the top of the world is intrinsically motivated to work hard toward that goal. The woman who trains to become a doctor simply because of the joy that healing brings her is also intrinsically motivated toward this achievement.

Extrinsic Motivation

Extrinsic motivation is the opposite. It's inspired by external factors, meaning you are pursuing a goal motivated by outside influences, specifically for an external reward. The person who climbs Mount Everest to have this "pinnacle of achievements" on his resume, for example, or to impress his friends is extrinsically motivated. The woman who trains to become a doctor for the prestige and the paycheck is extrinsically motivated.

As you may have guessed, writers whose impetus to write is to get rich and famous are extrinsically motivated to work toward these goals. Those who write for the joy it creates in their hearts are intrinsically motivated.

Examples of the Two Types of Motivation

Most writers are inspired by both types of motivation, but one is usually stronger than the other in driving them toward their goals. The intrinsically motivated writer may make the following types of comments:

- "It will feel so great to finish this novel. I just really believe in this story."
- "It's okay if my novel doesn't sell a lot of copies. I just feel great having it published."

- "I have tried to quit, but I can't. Writing is a compulsion I can't resist."
- "I love working on this book because I'm learning so much!"
- "This novel is the best I've ever written. I'm so proud of it, even if it never gets published."
- "Poetry fulfills me."
- "I love escaping into the lives of my characters."
- "This memoir has personal significance for me."

On the other hand, the extrinsically motivated writer may make these types of comments:

- "I can't disappoint my fans. I must finish this novel."
- "I'm thrilled my novel is selling so well."
- "My friends will be so impressed when they see I've published a novel."
- "Look, my byline is on a major website! My boss is going to freak out."
- "Once this book is published, people will take me seriously."
- "I was just taken on by a major New York agent. Surely now I'll get a big advance for my book."
- "I love that I can earn a full-time living from my writing. Getting that paycheck in the mail is the best!"
- "I'm hoping to win an award for this short story."
- "My client paid me to write this book, so I must do a good job."

Which Type Are You?

After reviewing the lists above, you may already have an idea which motivation is stronger for you. On the off chance you're still unsure, answer this one question: Starting today, if you never get published again—and for some reason, you are unable to self-publish—would you continue to write?

If your answer is "yes," you are more driven by intrinsic motivation. If it's "hmm, maybe not" or "no," you're more driven by extrinsic motivation. No matter which type you are, the important thing to remember is that intrinsic motivation leads to intrinsic rewards, and these are completely in your control. You don't have to rely on any outside forces to achieve them, which means you're likely to be successful—and that will give you the confidence you need to keep writing.

Extrinsic motivation, on the other hand, leads you to seek rewards from the outside world. Getting them, however, is out of your control. There's nothing wrong with going for them and they can indeed compel you to work hard. But if you fail to receive them, you may be more easily discouraged.

Intrinsic Motivation May Lead to Greater Creativity

In addition to being more in your control, there is evidence that intrinsic motivation may be more conducive to creative thought.

To test this connection, researcher Teresa M. Amabile of Brandeis University in Massachusetts chose seventy-two creative writing students and divided them into three groups. Then she had them participate in two sessions where they were asked to write two brief poems.

1. For the first session, all three groups were simply asked to write a poem.
2. For the second session, group one answered a questionnaire that focused on intrinsic motivations for writing before writing their poems. Group two answered a questionnaire that focused on extrinsic motivations for writing before writing their poems. Group three was a control group that answered no questionnaire before writing their poems.

The intrinsic motivation questionnaire consisted of statements such as these:

- You get a lot of pleasure out of reading something you've written.
- You achieve new insights through your writing.
- You like to play with words.

The extrinsic motivation questionnaire contained statements like these:

- You enjoy public recognition for your work.
- You have heard of cases where one bestselling novel or collection of poems has made the author financially secure.
- You realize that, with the introduction of dozens of magazines every year, the market for freelance writing is constantly expanding.

Twelve published poets then evaluated the poems. They found no differences in the poems written in the first session, but they did find differences in the poems written in the second one.

"Poems written under an extrinsic orientation were significantly less creative than those written in the other two conditions," the scientists wrote.

Other research has found similar results. In one study of twenty-nine professional artists who each submitted ten commissioned works and ten noncommissioned works, art experts consistently rated the noncommissioned works as more creative. Scientists theorized that the promise of an outside reward caused the artists to focus on the reward and took away some of the spontaneity that's so critical to creativity. It seems that anticipating a reward for a project diminishes the playfulness or experimentation with which you would approach it if you were doing it just for fun.

This is good news for those who are driven mostly by intrinsic motivation. But let's get real: Most of us are extrinsically motivated at least part of the time. We can't simply ignore that part—and we don't have to, because the best approach is to combine both motivation types when managing a lifelong writing career.

Fill the Gap with Achievable Goals

By focusing more on intrinsic rewards, you can fill in the Gap that a lack of extrinsic rewards may have created. But that doesn't solve everything. Intrinsic rewards alone can't be relied upon to completely fulfill us. Nor do they provide enough motivation to help us reach our highest potential. In the end, we need a little of both to become the best writers we can be.

Researchers have found this to be true with athletes. In their book *Inside Sport Psychology,* authors Costas I. Karageorghis and Peter C. Terry address intrinsic and extrinsic motivation as it relates to overall success:

"Our own research has shown that athletes who have the best motivational outcomes, such as persistence, a positive attitude, and unflinching concentration, tend to be both extrinsically and intrinsically motivated. Athletes who are predominantly extrinsically motivated tend to become discouraged when they do not perform to expectations and can experience a downturn in form. Conversely, athletes who are predominantly intrinsically motivated often do not have the competitive drive to become champions. This is because they tend to enjoy mastering the tasks that comprise their chosen discipline, but they lack a strong competitive streak in their personalities."

In my opinion, the same applies to writers. If you're doing this just for fun, then by all means focus solely on intrinsic motivation, and you'll be unlikely to be disappointed. But if your goal is to achieve professional status, make a living writing, or even just have your work read by readers, then you need some of each type of motivation to generate the drive that's necessary to succeed.

How This Works for Writers

Extrinsic motivation, for example, can inspire you to keep submitting to publishers, contests, and journals to gain recognition for your work. These submissions take time and effort; and if you aren't motivated to do it, your stories will likely remain in the drawer, unseen. Extrinsic motivation can also drive you to self-publish, start your own freelance writing business, or venture into public speaking.

All the while, intrinsic motivation is at work, keeping you going when external rewards are few. As Karageorghis and Terry state, "In the long run, extrinsic motivation is only effective when intrinsic motivation is high. Being driven solely by extrinsic motives is not psychologically healthy because the lack of intrinsic rewards can lead you to quit or seriously question your involvement. Having intrinsic motivation helps you get through dry patches in your career and keeps the emphasis on having fun."

Like so many things in life, it's a balancing act. Not only must we balance these two types of rewards and motivation, but we also need to rethink the types of outside rewards we're seeking. This is what I mean by setting more achievable goals. Many young writers shoot for the stars straight out of the gate, hoping for a byline in *The New Yorker* or a publishing contract with HarperCollins. Though these goals aren't impossible, they are improbable—particularly for a beginner—and not achieving them can lead to discouragement. Instead, it's better to modify the scale of the outside reward to align it with your experience and expertise in a way that allows gradual steps toward achieving your big dreams. So get a byline in a small online journal to start, or submit your work to a reputable indie publisher. Start small, and enjoy your rewards as you gain experience and reputation. Smaller steps stoke your confidence and motivation.

This brings us back to filling the Gap. Focusing more on intrinsic rewards will help, but so, too, will modifying your expectations of extrinsic rewards. Instead of hoping for bestselling status, focus on increasing the number of books sold between your first and second releases. Instead of hoping for a contest win, focus on improving the quality of your writing perhaps by hiring a mentor or book editor. Find ways to fill the Gap between work and reward by taking the following two steps:

1. Focus on intrinsic rewards, for these are entirely in your control.

2. Establish extrinsic rewards based on your personal progress rather than on lofty expectations modeled after famous writers.

I encourage you to do the following exercise before continuing to the next chapter. It will help you apply the two steps that are crucial to filling the Gap by thinking them through more carefully. As you go through the exercise, you'll be able to wrap your arms around the goals that are within your reach and more likely to encourage you to achieve, giving you a more motivating path forward in your writing career.

∽

Get the Rewards You're Shooting For

Vague goals don't get you where you want to go, so be clear on what you want from your writing. Start by jotting down as many intrinsic rewards as you can think of that you might like to achieve. Here are a few examples:

- Hold my first published book.
- Finish that special story.
- Complete that difficult novel, and prove to myself that I can do it.
- Create a new website that I'm proud of.

- Write an even better book than I did before.
- Practice writing thirty minutes a day just to feel the accomplishment.
- Master writing skills including characterization, setting, plot, dialogue, and story structure.

Next, narrow down your list to only the two intrinsic rewards that you feel are most significant for you and that you want to achieve in the next year. Write them down on a separate piece of paper.

Then, repeat this process with extrinsic rewards. Remember that it's best to gauge extrinsic rewards to where you are in your writing career right now. This makes them more attainable, which will motivate you to keep writing. Here are a few examples to get you thinking:

- Recruit X number of subscribers to my writing newsletter.
- Grow my social media following to 100 more *engaged* followers.
- Sell 20 percent more books with my next release than I did with my last one.
- Have one of my articles published by a small journal.
- Sign a publishing contract with a small indie publisher.
- Achieve recognition in a writing contest.
- Get a 5-star review on my book (or X number of 5-star reviews).
- Earn X amount of royalties with my books. (Keep it reasonable.)

Now, narrow your list down to the two extrinsic rewards that you feel are most significant for you and that you want to achieve in the next year. Write them down on the same piece of paper you used for your two intrinsic rewards, and post them somewhere you can see them. Then go for it, and see what you can accomplish.

The Many Benefits of Writing

*"I can shake off everything as I write;
my sorrows disappear, my courage is reborn."*

~Anne Frank

SIX

Why Can't We Just Write for Fun?

THINK BACK to when you started writing, to the very first time you opened a new Word file or pulled out a fresh piece of paper. Try to recall what was going through your mind. Chances are it had something to do with seeing your imaginary characters come to life, developing a creative idea, or simply wanting to play around with words for a while. Whatever it was, it's unlikely that it was about fame or money. In fact, I wager that the first few times you tried your hand at storytelling, you did it just for fun.

But a funny thing happens when we get serious about writing. It's not uncommon that, as writers progress, they lose the ability to be creative for creativity's sake and are plagued with worries about whether their time would be better spent on something else.

Later in this chapter, we'll explore the reasons why this happens. For now, let's examine the life experiences we may have that can tarnish the joy we get from writing and lead us to demand that we either produce a tangible result or stop fiddling around and do something worthwhile.

Creativity Gets Harder with Age

My younger brother is an artist. He'd laugh if he read that, but it's true. Hanging in my living room is a replica of the Starship Enterprise he created out of cardboard when he was a kid. It looks exactly like the real thing, particularly when the air currents in the room make it appear to be flying through space. On my writing desk is a toy van and trailer with a horse inside that he carved out of wood, the wheels pilfered from a Matchbox toy.

I always wished my brother had continued along this creative route as he got older, but he was drawn to working with machines and has spent most of his adult life fixing everything from cars and planes to trailers and lawnmowers. He's now expressing his creativity in this way, but perhaps one day he will return to the crafting that brought him joy as a child.

The ability to be creative comes naturally to us when we're young. It's "not" being creative that we have to learn. Author, speaker, and general systems scientist Dr. George Land discovered this in his research. In one particular study, he recruited 1,600 children who were enrolled in a Head Start program. He had them take the same creativity test he had designed for NASA's use in selecting innovative engineers and scientists. This test focused on the ability to come up with new and innovative ideas to solve problems. He tested the children between the ages of three to five, then re-tested them at age ten and again at age fifteen. Finally, he repeated the test on 280,000 adults.

The results showed something rather disturbing: children became *less* creative as they got older. Specifically, the proportion of children who had creative scores at the "genius" level was 98 percent among the three-to-five-year-olds, 30 percent among the ten-year-olds, and only 12 percent among the fifteen-year-olds. The kicker was that the adults tested at a dismal 2 percent.

As to why this happens, scientists have many theories. Land, however, feels that during the educational years, we make the big mistake of requiring young students to engage in two types of thinking simultaneously:

1. **Divergent Thinking**: Like brainstorming or imagining, this is where you come up with new ideas and ways of approaching a problem.
2. **Convergent Thinking:** This is when you test those ideas, judge their worth, and refine them to the point of usability.

The issue is that each type of thinking uses a different part of the brain and requires a completely different cognitive process. One (divergent) is like an accelerator, while the other (convergent) is the brake. Although it's important to learn to use both types of thinking to generate and evaluate creative ideas, each has its place and should occur at a different time.

Imagine any school or office setting where people are asked to come up with new ideas. The instant someone makes a suggestion, someone else often criticizes it or explains why it won't work. *That's crazy. We can't afford it. We can't get the materials.* Over time, we learn to react a certain way when asked to come up with new ideas. That is, we leap to judgment far too soon, essentially putting a huge stop sign in front of our imagination.

When observing what goes on inside the brain when both types of thinking are simultaneously required, researchers discovered that the neurons were fighting each other, diminishing thinking power "because we're constantly judging, criticizing, etc.," Land said in his TED Talk. These sorts of situations, repeated throughout childhood, teach us to immediately judge any original idea—and that kills creativity.

No wonder that when we adults feel compelled to write, we immediately judge those feelings and, similarly, prematurely judge any of the work we do. We're simply following what we've been taught—and, unfortunately, that keeps many adults from experiencing the joy that comes from creating.

Reawaken Your Love of Creativity

There are ways to unlearn the bad habits instilled in us during school and reawaken our love of creativity for creativity's sake.

1. You Don't Have to Be an Expert

Aspiring authors often worry that they lack the expertise to be taken seriously. "I can't write a book," a writer may say, "because I don't have a bunch of letters behind my name." By "a bunch of letters," these folks are usually referring to credentials like MD, PhD, and the like. Nonfiction writers feel this sort of pressure most keenly, but fiction writers are not immune.

I worried about this quite a bit. While I wanted to be a published novelist, I felt the dream was out of reach because I had no formal training. My bachelor's degree wasn't in writing. I thought of going back to get a master's degree in creative writing, but by the time the writing bug bit me, the cost of such a degree was more than I could manage.

I spent a lot of years thinking I had no business trying to be a serious writer because I was certainly no expert, and I've heard the same from other writers. Thankfully, many of us persevered and did just fine. So don't fall victim to this trap. There are many ways to educate yourself as you go that can help you improve your skills, and meanwhile, you are writing, which is the best teacher of all.

2. Don't Get Too Caught Up in Success versus Failure

Children never think about succeeding or failing. They just create because it's fun. As adults, however, we become far too sensitive to how others may judge our work, and thus the fear of failure looms large in our minds. This fear doesn't necessarily affect us while we're penning our stories (though it's easy to get caught up in fear early on), but it certainly does when it's time to show our work to others.

"Writing is such an intensely personal thing," wrote thriller author

Lori L. Robinett for Writing and Wellness, "it's daunting to release your work into the world. Though I dreamed of being a Writer (with a capital W), I struggled to overcome that fear that I wasn't good enough for a very, very long time. (Wait—who am I kidding? I still struggle with that!)"

There is perhaps nothing quite so frightening as giving a story you've agonized over to someone else to read, whether that person is a friend you hope not to alienate or an editor or agent you hope to impress. The answer is not to let fear of failure create a giant roadblock on your journey. Instead, see each failure as a learning experience (which it is!), and keep moving.

3. Don't Worry About Looking Good

Social media has created an intensified desire to look good in today's society. More than ever before, we're concerned with how we're seen, and not just physically. We create certain images of ourselves online and among our peers, and no one wants to look foolish. Yet what could be more ludicrous than putting out some story to which you don't know how people will respond?

This concern is a powerful deterrent to creativity. Entrepreneur and innovator Stephen Shapiro performed his own experiment while on a cruise to demonstrate this problem. He held a competition between adults and preteens, comparing how they reacted to a creative activity. "With the adults," Shapiro wrote in his blog, "this creative endeavor seemed like work. They were stiff, unfunny, and they were clearly thinking way too much about their responses. With the kids, everything flowed. They were funny, flamboyant, and outrageous. They did not censor their thoughts. They had no concern about looking silly."

Adults lose the ability to simply let loose. "We don't want to say something that might have us look bad in the eyes of our peers or boss," Shapiro writes. "This need to 'look good' stops us from playing."

This leads me to the next point.

4. Remember How to Play

In today's world, a child's life is likely to be filled with more structured activities designed to help them succeed than unstructured play. Thankfully, there has been recent pushback advocating for the power of play because it's important for optimal development.

In play, children learn to navigate physical and social environments, imagine and construct new realities, practice solving problems, and build new skills and interests. Play is so vital that the United Nations High Commission for Human Rights recognizes it as a right of every child.

Yogman and colleagues wrote in their study published in *Pediatrics*, "Play is not frivolous: it enhances brain structure and function and promotes executive function (i.e., the process of learning, rather than the content), which allow us to pursue goals and ignore distractions."

Adults, however, feel they are not really "supposed to play"—at least not too much. We have too many responsibilities to attend to; and besides, it's just not suitable for adults to chat with imaginary friends or play space invaders with Mattel toys. Yet people of all ages benefit from play. Certainly part of the pleasure of writing lies in engaging the inner child. This is often why writers feel guilty taking time away from other obligations to write. It feels so much like playing.

Yet we adults need to play if we want to live healthy lives. Research has shown that adults who play are happier, enjoy better cognitive and emotional health, and have a lower risk of developing age-related diseases like dementia. So unleash your inner child, laugh, and have fun!

5. Get Out of Your Rut

As we age, we tend to repeat the same routines and thought processes. If we're not careful, we can fall into a rut of rigid thinking that keeps the creative muse away. Instead, remember that creativity thrives on novelty. Children are always encountering new situations and experiences because they haven't been on the planet long. Adults, however, often get too comfortable in their familiar environments, and their number of new experiences dwindles year after year.

In a 2012 study, Simone Ritter and colleagues reported that unusual experiences increased cognitive flexibility or creativity more than the normal, day-to-day ones. New experiences force the brain to stop relying on neural shortcuts, opening up new pathways that spark creative ideas. I'm sure you'll agree that, in our adult lives, it's sometimes too easy to shun new experiences in favor of routine or familiar ones. To rekindle your creativity, do the opposite: get out and enjoy new experiences as often as you can.

6. Trust Yourself

If you're lucky, you have friends who encourage your creativity no matter what your age may be. Many adults aren't so fortunate, however. Their friends have jobs, families, and routine-driven lives. They talk about responsibilities, paying the bills, caring for the yard, and striving for that promotion. Start talking about how you're writing a story about vampires, and they may wonder what's wrong with you.

This comes back to the problem we talked about under Don't Worry About Looking Good. Part of the issue is about wanting to belong to a group. Unfortunately, indulging in a creative habit often sets you apart. It's not only the hours spent alone in a room writing, but also the fact that your friends may not understand *why* you'd want to do such a thing, especially when you have a job and three kids to take care of.

If we listen to others and care too much about their opinions—particularly those in our close social groups—we can easily find our creative aspirations dampened. Trust yourself. Feel free to hear your friend out, even if he thinks that vampire novel is a "silly" way of wasting time. If you agree, you can try something different. But if not, trust yourself and keep the creative juices flowing. Give in to others' opinions, and you could push creativity further out of your life.

7. Be Practical Only When It's Warranted

As adults, we are encouraged to be practical. Since that vacation to Hawaii is probably more than you can afford this year, you spend a couple of days at a nearby national park instead. Rather than sink your savings into a hot sports car, you get the used SUV that's large enough to carry the entire family. Adults learn that being practical is the way to happiness, as extravagance and whims often lead to regrets later on.

Unfortunately, creative endeavors are frequently viewed through this practical lens as well. There isn't much practicality to be had in spending hours every day on a story that may never go beyond your laptop, particularly if you consider yourself a wise adult. The key is to see beyond practical matters like making wholesome meals, fixing the leaking sink, and clearing out the clutter. Sure, when you finish these activities, you can see proof that you've made life better. But when you finish a story, you'll feel something entirely different—a feeling of fulfillment that can't be matched. Ask yourself which you'll be more proud of when you're eighty years old, then be sure to follow your priorities.

8. Don't Limit Your Abilities

Before being taught otherwise, children place no limits on what they believe they can accomplish. Ask kindergartners what they want to do when they grow up, and it's common to hear answers like being an astronaut, winning the Olympics, and becoming president of the United States.

By the time we reach adulthood, we have firm ideas about our limits and find it difficult to overcome some of them, which is normal. Unfortunately, this outlook can negatively affect our belief in our ability to develop as writers. We're too quick to imagine our limits rather than our possibilities and too slow to acknowledge our potential. There's no limit on what you can do as a writer, except the one that exists in your mind. Continue educating yourself, and see how much you can improve.

Indulge in Creativity—It's Not a Guilty Pleasure!

Many writers find their innate love of creativity stymied by guilt. Writer's guilt is such a pervasive problem that the term is highly popular on the Internet. (Go ahead. Google "writer's guilt," and you'll see.) It seems like taking time for creative pursuits feels selfish and unproductive to adults who think that practical activities like making money, caring for loved ones, cleaning the house, fixing things, and improving lives for ourselves and our families is time better spent.

Author Jodie Gibson describes creative guilt as "a feeling of remorse from spending time on creative pursuits with no defined outcome." Being creative, she writes, "or spending time on a creative pursuit is often dismissed as being fruitless. Worthless. Unproductive. A waste of time. Or my least favorite—a guilty pleasure."

This guilt can be so strong that it prevents adults from creating altogether. Talk about a destructive emotion! We can feel so compelled to write that we schedule it into our calendars, cancel other activities, and set up a space in which to do so. But then when it comes time to fill that blank page, we choke because we realize we're using our time to be creative. Who are we to think we can do that?

Friends and family often seem bent on returning us to the normal social order. They may show up in the middle of our scheduled writing time, bang on the door the instant we fall into our fictional dream world, or ask us point-blank what we hope to accomplish with "this writing thing." Indeed, it seems the instant we gather the courage to follow our dreams, those around us who aren't granting themselves the same gift become even more determined to drag us back to our practical-activities-only routine.

"The biggest emotional challenge for me as a writer is guilt," wrote author Natalie Bright for Writing and Wellness. "This emotion completely derails my forward momentum. It's as if I'm sneaking time to write in between day job, laundry, and cooking for a husband and our two boys."

Regardless of the messages we may have received while growing up—and those we continue to receive as adults about what creativity is and isn't—there's one thing that's clear from the research: engaging in creative activities is beneficial to our mental, emotional, and even physical health. All this nonsense about making sure we fill every minute of every day with productive, practical, non-creative activities is just that: nonsense.

Creativity Often Returns During the Golden Years

Despite how far we may wander from our innate creativity in adulthood, it's interesting how our natural love for creative play often returns as we get older.

After a difficult battle with throat cancer, actor Val Kilmer held the first showing of his artwork in 2017, having started to show his pieces on Twitter in 2014. He was an artist when he was a kid but left it behind while pursuing his acting career. When his throat cancer interfered with his ability to speak, he returned to the art he had enjoyed as a child.

Sir Anthony Hopkins also started painting late in life, after his wife saw his drawings and encouraged him to do so. He had enjoyed drawing as a child, and his mother had encouraged him. He was so accomplished that he even thought of becoming a commercial artist, but he told *W Magazine* that he was a "bad student" and couldn't take instruction. Now, he paints just for the fun of it. "Who would have thought after all those years I'd be painting?" he said. "I mean, life is full of surprises."

I don't think it's any big mystery why people who played with drawing, painting, and modeling as kids returned to it as older adults (though whether my brother will do so remains to be seen). The gift of creativity is valuable in and of itself, regardless of whether we earn anything from it. It fulfills us as nothing else can. What we understood instinctively as kids, we recall as seniors.

This may be because older adults often find themselves with fewer responsibilities. They may be retired. The kids are gone, too, so there's no need to take care of family. With extra time on their hands as well as a desire to break out of their daily routines, they return to the activities they loved as children.

I've interviewed many writers who have followed this path. They spent their lives in other occupations, then returned to writing during retirement because they had enjoyed it as kids.

"In the back of my mind," wrote author Mona Ingram for Writing and Wellness, "let's say since I was in my early teens . . . I'd imagined myself writing. As I got older, my favorite line became, 'My biggest decision will be what to wear on the Johnny Carson show.' Talk about expectations!"

As an adult, however, Mona tended to her day job, and her writing dreams moved to the back burner. "I did know one thing, however," she wrote. "And that was that I couldn't write while I was working, especially since I owned my own business, which took up almost every waking moment. But one day, shortly after I'd retired, I had purchased a romance [novel] by a big-name author—a really big name—and it read as though she'd phoned it in. That was the tipping point for me. I was convinced that I could do better."

Mona went on to write and publish several books. She, like many other writers who pursued their passion for writing despite all the challenges, proved that even though we may move away from our natural creativity as adults, it never really leaves us. All it requires is a little encouragement to come play with us once again.

Is Creativity Valuable on Its Own?

You may give lip service to creativity being valuable for creativity's sake, but truly believing it is an entirely different thing. Over the coming chapters, I want to convince you of the many reasons why your writing matters *no matter what happens with your work*. Though as adults we are hardwired to seek money, recognition, and other practical rewards—and the idea of spending time on an activity simply for its intrinsic benefits may seem foreign—often the most fulfilling lives are those spent pursuing something more.

As Tim Fizziar said (quoted in Francis Chan's book, *Crazy Love*),

"Our greatest fear should not be of failure . . . but of succeeding at things in life that don't really matter."

~

Discover Which Beliefs Are Holding You Back from Writing

Now that you're aware of the eight ways to reawaken creativity for creativity's sake, it's time to ask yourself which (if any) of these you need in your writing life right now. In your journal or notebook, write down the ones you need to work on to get your creativity humming again. Here's a quick roundup:

1. You don't have to be an expert.
2. Don't get too caught up in success versus failure.
3. Don't worry about looking good.
4. Remember how to play.
5. Get out of your rut.
6. Trust yourself.
7. Be practical only when it's warranted.
8. Don't limit your abilities.

Next, go through them one by one and ask yourself, "Do I want to keep thinking this way?" If not, try turning the statement around. Write it down on a Post-it® Note or another piece of paper.

The first one, for example, "I have to be an expert" becomes "I don't have to be an expert." The third one, "I want to look good" becomes "It doesn't matter if I look good." For some, you may need to take an extra step. With number five, for example, "I'm in a rut" could become "I'm getting out of my rut." Then give yourself three suggestions for how to do that.

See how you feel about these new statements. Hang up those that motivate you somewhere you can see them over the next couple of weeks. You may find that they spark new creative ideas about how you want to structure your writing life.

SEVEN

Writing to Heal

THE FIRST TIME I turned to writing, I was nine years old and looking for help. I was feeling bad about something (though I don't remember what), but I do remember going to my bedroom, shutting the door, and sitting on my bed, unsure of what to do with myself. Then I remembered the diary I'd recently received as a birthday present. It was a small journal with a white pearl-like cover. I held it in my hands and, even at that young age, felt something special about those blank white pages. I hadn't yet written in them, but that day I opened the drawer and there it was, that pretty little book with all the white pages inside. I got a pen and sat down at my desk with the first page opened in front of me. After a few moments, I started to write. Soon the words flowed, so I stuck with it until I got all my feelings out.

Over the next year or so, I filled every page in that diary. Whenever I finished writing, I would question what I'd written. Were my feelings right or wrong? Should I have them at all? But every time I finished writing and stashed the diary away, I felt better. Writing allowed me to share my true feelings without worrying that anyone would mock them. It was such a healing process that I became a dedicated journal writer for many years.

Later, as a health writer, it was no surprise when I discovered that freewriting—such as what one does in a diary—is a proven healer. It's probably the most popular reason people start writing in the first place, and a powerful reason why they continue with it.

Writing to Cope with Trauma and Loss

Expressive writing—writing to express feelings and emotions—has been studied extensively over the past few decades for its ability to provide healing benefits. On my motivational site, Writing and Wellness, I have featured many writers who were inspired to write their books because of personal trauma or loss.

Corporate executive Jo Ann Simon began writing after she lost her husband, Tom, to ALS (amyotrophic lateral sclerosis): "Afterwards, I decided to start writing about our beautiful life, as well as the rough and tough times, so that I would never forget. I was afraid that I would lose the details in time. Writing was the best medicine. It helped me immensely. It gave me a chance to realize what actually happened, instead of my denial of reality."

Writing was a way for Jo Ann to voice her feelings, as she went on to explain. "[It] was the only way to capture what we had. I didn't want to lose the wonderment of the short time we had together." Writing also allowed her to talk with her deceased husband in a way. "I wrote Dear Tom letters, which are in the book. They were a way for me to communicate with him to share my thoughts at that time. It is hard to be alone without your soul mate to talk to. Writing allowed me to communicate with him."

After realizing her story might help others who had experienced similar losses, Jo Ann decided to adapt her writing into book format. But what drew her to writing in the first place was her ability to express her feelings in a way that felt safe and supportive.

Psychologists have used logs, questionnaires, journals, and other forms of writing to help people heal from stresses and traumas for decades. As Joyce Hocker, PhD, wrote at *Psychology Today*, "Across many experiments, people experience a positive effect from employing expressive writing to cope with difficult life experiences. Even though a traumatic or grievous experience comes crashing into one's life unbidden, through writing, one can shape and explore the difficulty... . Taking time to write of one's own life experience provides a way to respect, hone and understand the trauma or loss."

Dr. James Pennebaker entered this area of research in the late 1980s and went on to conduct many studies on the subject. In his book, *Opening Up by Writing It Down*, he explained that expressive writing is a technique in which people write about an upsetting experience for fifteen to twenty minutes a day for three or four days. In his studies, he found this simple exercise improved people's physical and mental health for weeks, months, and even years compared to individuals who wrote about neutral topics that inspired no emotion.

Expressive writing also helps people to overcome depression and anxiety. In a 2013 study, scientists found that patients who were diagnosed with major depressive disorder (MDD) and wrote about their deepest thoughts and feelings for twenty minutes over three consecutive days showed significant decreases in depressive scores compared to those who simply wrote about the events of their days. Four weeks later, the benefits were still there.

Similarly, Lujun Shen and colleagues discovered that long-term expressive writing (every day for thirty days) helped reduce test anxiety in college students. John Pachankis and Marvin Goldfried reported in 2010 that expressive writing targeting gay-related stress improved gay men's psychosocial functioning, especially openness with sexual orientation. And in a 2005 study, Karen Baikie and colleagues acknowledged that writing about traumatic events improved physical and psychological health—so much so that they recommended expressive writing as a therapeutic tool for survivors of trauma and in psychiatric settings.

Regular expressive writing may even provide relief from chronic worrying. Hans S. Schroder and colleagues tested expressive writing in chronic worriers and compared their outcomes to a control group. The results showed that those who wrote about their feelings were able to offload them onto the page, thereby reducing anxiety and relieving stress.

Why Writing Helps

Researchers have several theories explaining why writing helps with emotional and mental difficulties. One is that writing about an experience—along with expressing emotions—organizes thoughts, which, in turn, helps create meaning out of trauma. It's common after experiencing a difficult time or suffering the loss of a loved one to want to make sense of what happened. We need to know why this happened and what to do now. Writing helps us face the facts of what occurred and allows us to get a better grip on our feelings about the experience itself, freeing us to figure out our next steps.

A second theory suggests that when we write, we create a story out of the experience. This engages the intellectual side of the brain, which helps break the cycle of unhealthy brooding that often occurs after trauma. In writing a story, we intellectually confront what happened, process it, and heal. The story becomes a part of us, something we can use as a source of strength rather than weakness.

Jo Ann experienced something like this after writing her book. "I was inspired by doing this," she wrote, "and it felt like a tribute to Tom in the beginning, but then it changed to be about us and then me and how I could live my life again. It was healing for me. . . . Once the book was published, I could live in the present and look forward to the next chapter in my life, and to writing my next book."

A third theory suggests that simply opening up about an experience encourages further expression, which leads to sharing with others and finding the social support needed to fully recover. Author Beth Castrodale experienced this sort of benefit when writing about losing her parents. "In late 2014 and early 2015," she wrote for Writing and Wellness, "my elderly parents died within four months of each other. Although their deaths were far from unexpected, I found myself unable to forge ahead on the novel I'd been working on over the previous two years. Against the loss of my parents, the novel felt trivial. Furthermore, grief diminished my ability to concentrate and to devote to the novel the close attention it required. So I set it aside."

Instead of abandoning writing entirely, however, Beth used it to help her manage her suffering from these losses: "Thus, instead of allowing grief to get in the way of my writing, I let it become a subject of my writing, exploring loss through short works of fiction and nonfiction. Over the months that followed, this strategy helped me cope with the emotions surrounding the deaths of my parents, allowing me to get back on track with my novel."

Writing Benefits Your Physical Health, Too

Research on expressive writing has gone beyond emotional and mental health. In fact, some of the earliest studies on the practice showed clear *physical* benefits. In one of Pennebaker's first experiments, he had one group of participants write about their deepest feelings concerning a past trauma, while a control group simply wrote about superficial or neutral topics. Both groups wrote for fifteen minutes a day for four consecutive days. He also measured the participants' immune function at the start and end of the study.

Results showed that the participants who poured out their feelings had improved immune-system functioning and made fewer visits to the health center in the following months compared to those who wrote superficially. This outcome was surprising at the time, but several studies since then have added evidence to the connection between writing and physical well-being.

For their experiment, Annette Stanton and colleagues divided early-stage breast cancer patients who were completing medical treatment into three groups. Over the course of four sessions, each group was asked to write the following:

1. **Group 1:** Their deepest thoughts and feelings regarding breast cancer
2. **Group 2:** Their positive thoughts and feelings regarding their experience with breast cancer
3. **Group 3:** The facts of their breast cancer experience

The scientists then assessed the women's psychological and physical health at one and three months after the experiment. After three months, those in group 1 reported significantly decreased physical symptoms, and those in groups 1 and 2 had significantly fewer medical appointments for cancer-related illnesses.

It seems that expressive writing can also have a direct effect on the immune system, although exactly how it may boost healing is still unknown. The effects, nonetheless, can be quite startling. In 2017, scientists recruited 122 healthy participants between the ages of eighteen and fifty-five and randomly assigned them to perform expressive writing or neutral writing either before or after receiving a four-millimeter punch biopsy wound. They then photographed the wounds on days ten and fourteen to measure healing.

Results showed significant differences in healing. At day ten, those who performed expressive writing before the biopsy had fully healed wounds compared to those who had performed neutral writing either before or after being wounded. The scientists concluded that expressive writing could improve healing if performed *before* wounding. They added that expressive writing *after* wounding could also help if performed within a few days of the injury.

Earlier research found similar effects on patients with asthma and rheumatoid arthritis. Joshua Smyth and colleagues asked patients to write about the most stressful event of their lives or emotionally neutral topics for twenty minutes a day, three days in a row. All patients were examined at the start of the study, then again at two weeks, two months, and four months after writing.

Results showed that the asthma patients who wrote about stressful events improved their lung function from 63.9 percent at the start of the study to 76.3 percent at the four-month follow-up. The control group, which wrote about emotionally neutral topics, showed no change. The rheumatoid arthritis patients in the experimental group showed a 28 percent overall improvement in disease activity at the four-month follow-up, whereas the control group experienced no change. When the results were combined, nearly half of the experimental patients experienced clinically relevant improvements, compared to less than a quarter of the control patients. The researchers concluded that the improvements were beyond those attributable to the standard medical care that all the patients were receiving.

Similar patterns were also seen among patients with HIV/AIDS. Participants spent four thirty-minute sessions writing about negative life experiences or their daily schedules. Afterward, those who wrote about emotional experiences tested higher in immune functioning than those who wrote about their daily schedules. Scientists believed the immune boosts occurred because of the stress- and anxiety-relieving effects of the writing periods.

Expressive writing has even been found to help stressed-out healthcare workers. In one 2017 study, scientists found that writing made it easier for employees to cope with changing situations, improved communications among workers, and increased cognitive function.

Writers Write to Heal, Whether They Know It or Not

In my interviews with other writers, I find that most turn to writing, at least in part, for its healing potential, whether or not they are aware of it. When writing her first book, African author Jane Nannono noted, "The writing itself was cathartic—freeing and therapeutic. It helped me get to know myself at a deeper level. I became more sensitive to my feelings and emotions and opened myself up to being more human."

Literary author Patty Somlo had a similar experience, an unconscious knowing that writing could heal. "I loved the moment when, after hours of research and interviews, I got to write," she wrote for Writing and Wellness. "As someone who had unknowingly suffered from depression and anxiety for years, it was a relief to be able to lose myself in writing."

Many writers have found a more direct route to healing through writing as well. Author Rebecca Whitehead Munn was reeling with her mother's diagnosis of terminal cancer when she chose writing. "Some days felt like quicksand, others like water," she wrote for Writing and Wellness. "Writing about my experience provided a sort of therapeutic outlet, a place where I could pour out my heart and feel somewhat relieved, versus feeling judged by someone who was hearing my story."

The process of writing a book, in particular, seems to provide a unique type of relief. As Pennebaker noted in his studies, when we seek to create stories out of our experiences, we go through a process of bringing our emotions out where we can see them and deal with them, and gradually we find meaning in those experiences and thereby gain some peace.

"Many times, I cried my way through a chapter and would have to stop and recover," wrote Christian author Rebecca Olmstead for Writing and Wellness, referring to writing a book about her cancer experience. "I was recovering physically from my ordeal, but writing *Loved So Much It Hurts*, a two-year journey, allowed my soul to heal as well."

She went on to note that it was later in the process of preparing the book for publication that she could see how far she had come: "My biggest triumph came in editing the book. When I clearly saw the path this ordeal led me on, from being broken to recognizing the flaws in my self-image, to being set on my true life's path. That was when I realized the purpose in my pain...."

There are many more similar stories told by writers as well as those who do not consider themselves writers per se but felt compelled to write to deal with trauma and loss. Certainly thirteen-year-old Anne Frank wrote in her diary for the same reasons when recording the difficulties she and her family faced in German-occupied Amsterdam. She wasn't looking for fame and fortune, though she did hope to be a journalist one day. But as to the purpose behind her devotion to her diary, she wrote, "When I write I can shake off all my cares. My sorrow disappears, my spirits are revived!"

Do You Write to Heal?

To find out if healing is one of the benefits you gain from writing (and one of the reasons why your writing matters), answer the following questions using a scale of 0 to 5, with 5 meaning "almost always" and 0 meaning "never."

_____ I find writing therapeutic.
_____ After writing, I usually feel better.
_____ I feel healthier overall when I'm writing regularly, even if just in a journal.
_____ I often turn to writing when I'm dealing with difficult emotions.
_____ Writing helps me process and understand my life in general.

Your total score: _____

13 or higher: Healing is frequently a benefit of writing for you.
13 or lower: Healing may not be one of the benefits of writing for you.

Seven Tips for Using Expressive Writing to Heal

It doesn't matter whether you are a seasoned writer or a beginner. Taking time out of your schedule to engage in expressive writing can be healing. Even though this writing may or may not lead to a new story or novel, what's important is that you enjoy the healing benefits that writing brings and remind yourself of the many ways writing matters in your life.

Though any type of expressive writing is likely to be helpful, some methods seem to be more effective. To increase your chances of healing, use the following tips:

1. **Write in a series of sessions.** Go for ten to twenty minutes per day for at least three to four days. You can also make it a daily practice if you like.
2. **Write about your feelings.** You can start by writing about your day, but be sure to always get into how you *feel* about what happened. Getting your feelings down on paper opens the door to healing.
3. **Narrow your focus to one event.** Choose one event that was difficult or emotional for you, and focus on it during your writing sessions for the week. You can always choose another event to focus on at another time.
4. **Ask yourself why.** Why are you experiencing these emotions? Where are they coming from? Do they relate to an experience you had in the past?

5. **Build to writing a story.** The object is not to write a story about an emotional event. But if you can gradually work toward that, the writing will likely be more helpful than if you continue only to write about your feelings. Be careful not to get stuck in a negative pattern. Once you've written down how you feel—it's okay if it takes several days—then shift into developing it into a story.
6. **Don't criticize this writing.** Trust in the privacy of your writing. You don't have to share it unless you want to, which means there's no reason to judge it. Just write and let it be what it is. Even if you make the move to writing a story, don't judge its quality. Allow the process of writing to work its healing magic on you.
7. **Write from another perspective.** After four to five days of writing about an experience, if you don't want to make it into a story, try writing about it from another person's perspective. It could be either someone else you know or—better yet—a made-up character. Allowing another entity to tell your story can be very freeing.

EIGHT

Writing to Escape

ESCAPE IS one of writing's most celebrated pleasures. I can speak from experience about those magical days when everything flows. I find myself living in the world my characters inhabit, diving so deeply into this alternative universe that, when I surface, I'm often surprised to discover how much time has gone by. Sometimes we writers simply want to go somewhere else, do something else, or *be* someone else. The more experienced we become at our craft, the more adept we get at disappearing into our stories.

As English novelist Graham Greene wrote, "Writing is a form of therapy; sometimes I wonder how all those who do not write, compose, or paint can manage to escape the madness, melancholia, the panic and fear which is inherent in a human situation."

Why This Fascination with Escape?

It's easy to see how financial hardships, family strife, illness, and other issues can make the daily grind too much to take. Add to that the near-constant stream of negative news coming at us these days, and you can see why anyone would want to get away for a while.

According to a 2017 survey of around 2,000 people, respondents spent an average of nearly thirteen hours each week escaping their reality. Writers will be happy to know that about one-and-a-half of those weekly hours were spent reading books, with about two-and-a-half hours spent watching movies and about forty-five minutes dreaming of vacation. Other popular forms of escape included exploring new places and listening to music.

It seems we are a nation seeking escape. During difficult times—such as after 9/11 or during the COVID-19 pandemic—escapism can even become a form of self-care. For many people, movies provide a satisfying solution to a troubling situation as the hero rises triumphant or the victim gets justice. Movies also take us to places we've never been and allow us to imagine ourselves as different people. They help us virtually explore the world while escaping our problems for an hour or two, transporting us to more enchanting realities than our own. In the real world, we often feel powerless to make things right. But in a movie or book, we can take up our swords and shields and ride into battle, knowing we're likely to emerge victorious. When writing, we often enjoy even more of a sense of rightness as we create worlds where things turn out like we think they should.

Finding a way to escape from real life helps us avoid further distress and psychological harm. Escape is a coping mechanism, a method of gaining calm and tranquility so we can rally the inner strength we need to face our daily challenges. And though there are many ways to escape, writing is arguably one of the most creative, productive, and healthy options.

Writing: The Healthy Escapism

Writing is a positive form of escape because it helps us hone our skills, become more empathetic, enjoy a healthy form of distraction, and improve our quality of life. Let's look at each of these benefits more closely.

Writing Helps Us Hone Our Skills

To write a publishable novel, you have to learn a *lot* about writing, editing, publishing, and marketing. This process can take years. In fact, it can take the rest of your life, which is one of the reasons why writing is so satisfying: you never stop learning.

Through the process of trial and error, writing and rewriting, working with mentors, publishing books, blogging, interacting with readers, writing more books, publishing more books, taking classes, and attending conferences, you gradually develop into a more accomplished writer. Few other forms of escape provide such powerful developmental effects.

On top of that, few skills are as beneficial as writing. Developing the ability to write well—even if you never become a bestseller—helps you master communication skills that can be applied to other areas of your life, particularly on the job. A survey of employers conducted by the Association of American Colleges and Universities found that the majority of employers looked for candidates with "the ability to effectively communicate orally and in writing."

The National Writing Project, a professional development network that serves teachers of writing at all levels, also surveyed business leaders and found that as "advanced technology in the workplace plays a more significant role, good writing skills are increasingly valued by big business." Writing was considered a threshold skill, the investigators found, and a "ticket to professional opportunity." As one executive noted, "[T]he need to write clearly and quickly has never been more important than in today's highly competitive, technology-driven global economy."

As long as you focus on improving your writing skills while you're escaping into your stories, the benefits you gain will show up outside of your writing life, seeping into your professional and personal life as what you've learned in your isolated writing nook improves your communication with others.

Writing Helps Us Become More Empathetic

As you wrestle with plotlines and character arcs, you're also learning how to empathize with your characters, even the antagonistic ones. To create authentic people on the page, you need to imagine how it would be to live someone else's life, including someone completely different from you. Writers spend hours upon hours living as their characters until, eventually, we know them as well as we do ourselves. It's not uncommon for a writer to cry after killing off a character or feel elated when the hero saves the day.

Writing and reading are complementary activities; and studies show that the more we read, the more compassionate we become because of our connection to the characters in the story. Fiction readers score higher in measures of empathy and theory of mind (the ability to think about others' thoughts and feelings) than non-readers. In 2015, Diana Tamir and colleagues reported, "Recent research in psychology suggests that readers make good citizens because reading may improve one's ability to empathize with and understand the thoughts and feelings of other people."

The more readers become immersed in a story, the more they care about the characters and what happens to them. This type of immersion is associated with increased empathy. In one study, scientists tested a group of people to see if this effect would translate into more empathetic or caring actions.

First, they asked the participants questions to measure empathy. Next, they had these same participants read a short story and answer questions about the extent to which they'd gotten immersed into the story. For example, could they picture the characters and where they were? And did they want to learn more about those characters after finishing the story?

Finally, the scientists left the room and, on the way out, dropped a handful of pens. Those participants who were more immersed in the story they'd read were more likely to help retrieve the pens. A follow-up experiment showed that those who felt immersed in the characters' lives also had a higher likelihood of engaging in prosocial (i.e., helpful) behavior. What's even more telling is that these results held regardless of the person's tendency to be empathetic (as measured in the original questionnaire), suggesting that reading the story had a definite positive effect.

As writers of fiction, we have an even greater chance of growing more empathetic through our work because we—perhaps even more so than our readers—get completely absorbed in our characters' lives. They are like real people to us because we know them so well. We inhabit their worlds, interact with them, go on adventures with them, and witness their challenges. We *are* them for a time, which can permanently change us once the story is done.

"There were years between that my story went untouched," wrote fantasy author Sara Secora for Writing and Wellness. "However, the story, and more importantly, the characters, were never far from my mind. In a way, I grew into my adulthood along with the characters inhabiting the world of Vataenya."

Writing Is a Healthy Form of Distraction

Meanwhile, while you're in that other world and becoming more empathetic, you can escape from your realities in a positive way. As long as you're not using writing to avoid your regular life for too long, you can gain distance from your problems and allow yourself some respite—and perhaps an adventure with a dragon along the way.

Though expressive writing can be healing, as I noted in chapter 7, ruminating over your problems is not always the best way to deal with them. One study that allowed participants to use a punching bag to blow off steam found they actually experienced *greater* levels of anger afterward than those who did nothing at all. A distraction—particularly, writing—can be much more effective in diffusing volatile situations or managing difficult emotions.

I know I'm not alone in emerging from a writing session feeling a lot better than when I started. I have difficult writing days, too. But most of the time, if I succeed in diving deep into the underwater world that is my imagination, I surface with more energy and a brighter outlook.

"The great thing about writing is that you create a make-believe world," wrote mystery writer Ilene Birkwood for Writing and Wellness, "a place where you can forget your problems and relax. My husband had leukemia and endured two years of chemotherapy before he passed away. I used to drive him to a clinic every few days where they pumped him full of drugs. Watching him suffer without being able to do anything about it was truly terrible—as so many of you must know. When we arrived home, I made him comfortable in bed or in front of [the] TV and escaped into the wonderful therapeutic world of my book. Wrapped up in the plot, I relaxed for the first time in hours."

Instead of always venting difficult emotions, it's often better to distract yourself by getting involved with something else. The wonderful thing about writing is that it's so *constructive*. Writers build and create something that one day is of value to another. What better coping mechanism could we ask for?

Writing Improves Our Quality of Life

To be engaged in any activity you enjoy is a healthy way to distract yourself—as long as the activity contributes rather than subtracts from your quality of life. When listing healthy forms of escape, psychologists often include activities like yoga, listening to music, exercising, traveling, engaging in a hobby, spending time with a pet, or going out with friends and loved ones. The idea is to do something you enjoy to feel better. Just don't use the activity to avoid your problems.

Escaping in a healthy way, though, is not always easy in today's world. There are so many forms of entertainment available that make it much too easy to flee problems than to face them. In a 2016 study, researchers found that senior high school students who were suffering from psychological distress were more likely to turn to the Internet and engage in online activities to get away from their lives. These students also ran a greater risk of developing a psychologically harmful Internet dependency.

One can't examine the dangers of unhealthy technological escapism without considering the smartphone. Studies abound about its addictive tendencies and how distracting it can be even when it's merely sitting nearby because we're always thinking about the messages, texts, likes, and other satisfying goodies it may hold for us. Unfortunately, those who fall victim to its mesmerizing hits of dopamine soon find their anxiety levels rising. Research shows that the more time we spend on those gadgets, the more anxious and depressed we're likely to be.

As speaker Werner Schouten wrote on LinkedIn, "Increased phone use results in more self-escapism causing people to refrain more and more from introspection as our minds are not given the time to critically investigate *what* we are feeling. Introspection is imperative for people in order to understand the meaning of the world around them better and to find opportunities for improvement of oneself in this world. Excessive phone use hinders this process of understanding our complex society and our own place in this society."

On the contrary, writing often encourages reflection and helps writers to *better* understand themselves. I don't think I knew myself very well at all until I had been writing for a few years. Other writers have expressed similar experiences.

Wrote award-winning author and writing mentor K. M. Weiland on Helping Writers Become Authors, "You must have a relationship with your stories before your readers can, and really this is a relationship with yourself. In recognizing this, writing becomes both an investigative tool for getting to know yourself better and a vast playground for exploration and experimentation on a deeply personal level."

I'll go into this relationship of writing for self-discovery in more detail in chapter 12, but I wanted to mention it here as one of the reasons why writing is a healthy form of escape. Unlike other activities that help us avoid ourselves, writing often does the opposite: it holds up a metaphorical sort of mirror, allowing us to see ourselves more clearly.

As fantasy author Kai Raine wrote for Writing and Wellness, "Somehow, in letting go and learning to love each of these characters not despite their flaws but with them, I learned to love those parts of myself, too. In a way, over the course of writing this book, I came to know myself better, and to love all these different facets of myself."

Do You Write to Escape?

To find out if escape is one of the benefits you gain from writing (and one of the reasons why your writing matters), answer the following questions using a scale of 0 to 5, with 5 meaning "almost always" and 0 meaning "never."

_____ I can get so involved in my writing that I lose track of time.

_____ When the world gets too crazy, I love to escape into my stories.

_____ I often think about my characters and am eager to get back to their lives.

_____ I sometimes prefer my story worlds to the real one.

_____ After an intense writing session, I often feel better than I did before writing.

Your total score: _____

13 or higher: Escape is likely a frequent benefit of writing for you.
13 or lower: Escape may not be one of the benefits of writing for you.

Is Your Method of Escape Healthy?

To determine if your escapism is healthy, ask yourself if any of the following are true:

- My escapism is hurting my job and/or my relationships.
- I'm displaying addictive behaviors. For example, I feel uneasy if I have to be away from my preferred escape method for too long.
- I frequently procrastinate about important things so I can escape—to the point of experiencing problems.
- I engage in my escapist activity whenever I feel difficult emotions that I have yet to deal with.
- My form of escape is hurting my health.
- Others tell me that I'm spending too much time on my form of escape.
- I feel worse or the same (but not better) after escaping.

If you answered "untrue" to most of these statements, then your form of escape is working. If you answered "true" to even one statement, though, it's time to consider a healthier form of escape, like writing a story.

If you worry that you're escaping too often into your writing—perhaps you're chronically late for work, or it's hurting your relationships—consider why. Maybe you don't like your job, and you're using your writing to avoid it. Or maybe you're avoiding an aspect of your relationship by escaping into your writing.

Journal about how you feel for a few days. Chances are you'll find the answer. Meanwhile, remember that writing is overall a wonderful method of escape with many health benefits.

NINE

Writing to Discover the Truth

FOR AS LONG AS I can remember, I've wrestled with the big questions in life. Even as a child, I would look out my window and wonder, *Why am I here? Where did I come from?* I felt a spiritual connection to something then, but I couldn't define what it was.

I continue to seek information in research, spiritual practices, journaling, and meditation, but it is in my stories that I find the most satisfying "answers." There, I can explore the big questions that have always plagued me like, *What happens after we die?* This question was the one I wrestled with in my novel *Loreena's Gift*.

I lost an extremely important person in my life when I was only four years old. Looking back now, I can see how much I struggled to make sense of it. Children often can't speak logically about their emotions. I certainly couldn't then. Instead, my feelings came out in strange ways. I used to sit at the table and punch my stomach, for instance, which seemed to me to be a perfectly normal thing to do. My family thought differently and would ask me why I was doing that. "My stomach hurts," I'd answer. My siblings would make fun of me. "Yeah, your stomach hurts because you're punching it!" I had no answer to that, so I would stop punching for a few minutes but soon be back at it again.

I know now that my stomach muscles were tight from anxiety, and punching them was my way of easing the tension. The anxiety was related to the loss I'd experienced, the changes that happened as a result, and my confusion about it all, as well as my concern about whether things were going to be all right from that point on. My mom worked hard to provide a stable life for us, and soon I grew out of that early anxiety. But the question remained.

What happens when we die?

It wasn't until I wrote *Loreena's Gift* that I was finally able to dive into this question with all the passion I had built up over the years. I didn't even realize what I was doing at first. I'm a pantser by nature—I don't outline my stories—so I was just writing away when suddenly I realized my main character, Loreena, had the power to kill people with a touch of her hand. Before the person died, though, my heroine would travel with them to the afterlife, which would be however the person imagined it, good or bad.

By following Loreena through her adventures, I was able to explore many different possibilities for what the afterlife might (or might not) look like, which I found incredibly satisfying on many levels. Writing not only helped me find the answers I was looking for, so to speak, but also gave me the means to live through various possibilities via my main character. Somehow, that brought me peace.

Writing is unique among the arts because it encourages us to ask the big questions and then explore a variety of answers. "I think when we write," said American novelist and playwright Adam Rapp in *The American Theater Reader*, "we aspire to ask big questions, and when we don't it just becomes an exercise."

If this sounds familiar to you, consider that your writing matters because it gives you a way to figure things out. Your questions may not be as heavy as mine, but whatever they are, they are important enough for you to explore. Writing gives you that wonderful opportunity to create your own world and play out various scenarios in search of answers. By doing so, it increases your understanding of yourself and the people around you. No wonder so many writers enjoy spending time plunged deep into their stories. It's like having a personal holodeck where you get to choose the program you want to experience and then see where it takes you.

We Rarely Reflect on the Big Questions Today

Sadly, modern life allows little time to reflect on the big questions. Instead, more importance is placed on status, money, success, and comfort. Because we are taught to think of these things as priorities, we work our fingers to the bone for a paycheck that doesn't even come close to providing them all, but we keep chasing after them anyway.

To ponder the big questions, we need time, space, and quiet—and as I'm sure you know, there's little of that to be had today. Between work, family, caring for a household, and community responsibilities, we barely find the time to get in seven to eight hours of sleep per night (say nothing of pondering why we're here or what might be the meaning of life). Yet we should wrestle with these questions at some point. If we don't, we're likely to follow society's path like sheep rather than making our own path in the world.

"Are the Big Questions . . . irrelevant today?" asked Bill Noblitt, editor of *Stetson Magazine*. "Is there no place left to use our reason to ponder the meaning of love and desire; living a virtuous life; creating an ideal government; understanding truth, goodness, beauty and the nature of evil . . . ?"

Don't wait too long to ponder these questions. Resist floating along passively on life's momentum until you reach your golden years, when things finally slow down and you wonder how it all went by so fast. This is when the regrets settle in.

"It's no wonder so many of us fail seriously to ponder life's big questions until our twilight years, when the pace of life finally slows down," wrote Jim Loehr in his book *The Only Way to Win: How Building Character Drives Higher Achievement and Greater Fulfillment in Business and Life*. "Unfortunately, by then so much time has passed, so many growth opportunities have been missed, so little time is left on our biological clocks."

Every day, each of us makes a huge decision: how to live life. You owe it to yourself to make that decision thoughtfully and purposefully, rather than simply doing what you've been taught or what you see others doing. Instead, carefully think about the sort of life that will be uniquely fulfilling for you. Pondering this isn't just a nice thing to do while taking a long drive. Your ultimate decision could make the difference between a satisfying or unsatisfying life.

The Big Questions Come Up After Loss

It's no surprise that a personal loss triggered my own big questions. When life is shaken to the core by loss, trauma, illness, natural disaster, or other similar earth-shattering events, it shakes us up and forces us to face life in its entirety—for a moment at least. When life is normal, we tend to see only the day ahead. But after a shocking experience upends everything, we naturally look further down the road, both in the direction of where we're going and where we've been. The things that seemed so important only days before now seem inconsequential. All of a sudden, it makes no difference whether the house is clean and organized. That upcoming promotion doesn't seem like such a big deal. Loss and trauma reduce us to the very fragile beings we are and force us to *deal* with this thing called life.

It is during times like these that writers turn to the page. We want to know why this particular event occurred. Writing allows us to explore it in a healthy way, which is a blessing. Without that outlet, we can suffer enduring grief and pain without knowing how to find relief.

Author Crissi Langwell was twenty-four years old when she experienced a stillbirth. "At 32 weeks along in my pregnancy," she wrote for Writing and Wellness, "we discovered the baby's heartbeat had stopped. This was something I never imagined was even possible. I mean, I had heard about it happening to other parents, but those stories seemed so far away from me."

As with so many, the trauma turned Crissi's life upside down. "When it happened to us, it changed everything I knew about life. I went into a deep, dark depression and had a hard time caring for my living children, or even myself. My once clean house became a pit. The demise of my marriage accelerated (we were already having problems), and we divorced soon after."

What helped Crissi was writing a novel about the loss of a child. *"The Road to Hope* was my opportunity to write about this loss and its effects on my life," she wrote, "channeling my grief through Jill, one of the main characters. Then I introduced another character, a teen mom named Maddie, who allowed me to write about other experiences in my life—poverty and being a young mother, and in later books, domestic violence and identity issues. So, *The Road to Hope* started as a story, but it became so much bigger than that."

By the time she finished her book, Crissi had moved through her grief to a greater acceptance of herself. "Writing *The Road to Hope* allowed me to work through some really hard emotions, things I'd held on to for years. It gave me grace for the person I was, even love for that earlier version of myself, because I was able to see it from a bigger point of view."

That's the beauty of writing. Living through scene after scene as our characters—all while simultaneously existing in the characters around them—gives us the ability to transform our usual singular point of view to a much broader perspective. Though we may not find answers to the big questions such as "Why does an innocent child die?", we can find healing in exploring the question with our friends on the page.

Author Elaine Mansfield lost Vic, her dear husband of forty-two years, to lymphoma in 2008. She described him as her "confidante, spiritual companion, and best friend." Though she'd always been a writer, his illness and eventual loss compelled her to turn to the page more often.

"My journals became factual and emotional records of Vic's illness," she wrote for Writing and Wellness. "When I was exhausted, frightened, or angry, I let my feelings loose on the pages. After Vic's death, I felt an inner impulse to turn the chaotic feelings into stories."

Writing helped Elaine heal, and initially, that was enough. But she wanted to go further. "In the beginning, I wasn't writing a book. I was writing to find meaning and to objectify what I'd seen and felt. After a few years of writing short pieces, I realized I had the bones of a book."

Elaine joined a class to learn more about memoir writing and then published her book, *Leaning into Love*, in 2014. "I knew I needed to turn toward grief rather than running from it, and writing helped me do that. I want people to know that even after shattering experiences, they can find joy again if they look for it."

Writing to Discover the Truth

Gautama Buddha is credited with saying, "Find out for yourself what is truth, what is real." This is also why many writers write. Fiction teaches us more about our own stories and the stories of those around us. But it's the process of writing that reveals the truth.

"During the course of the last couple of years of struggling with the story I was also grappling within myself," wrote speculative fiction author Ian Acheson for American Christian Fiction Writers. "Having completed the first draft early in the year I was able to reflect a little on the process. What became apparent was I needed to go through my own season of discovery about myself to be able to write the story."

Authors often begin a story with a question they're wrestling with. This may be a "why" question or something they're struggling with personally. By being patient and sticking with the difficult process that novel writing often is, authors eventually arrive not where all the answers are, but rather at a better place where they are more at peace.

"I believe that's why the latest story is often the hardest one even if you've written fifty of them," Acheson wrote. "Because you don't know what you're going to learn about yourself when you're writing it. We write stories to discover the truth."

Maybe you've heard your writing teachers or mentors tell you to "write the truth." It separates the pros from the wannabes—and of course, we want to go pro. But what exactly does it mean to write the truth?

What It Means to Write the Truth

Simply put, write what you know. You've likely heard this a million times. Unfortunately, it's frequently misinterpreted as writing only about personal experiences. But that doesn't serve most writers well, particularly those who enjoy indulging their imaginations. Writing what you know is more about focusing on the truth of what you've experienced. Think of it this way: What do you know about loss? Hurt? Triumph? Struggle? We have all experienced a wide range of human emotions, and writing honestly about them is the best way to unearth the truth in your writing.

"Writing what you know is getting to the core of yourself," wrote author and artist Amanda Stockton on her blog, *Batwords Media*. This, she adds, is often why writing can be so difficult, slow, and stagnant. But for those who can stick it out, the rewards are often well worth it. "Writing your truths in fiction is freedom. Even in the pain that can be carried along with that. . . . It won't make the thing go away, but it may reduce its power over you. Or, if nothing else, you'll extend a lifeline to someone else who felt isolated in themselves."

It's funny how writing fiction—often more than nonfiction—makes it easier to uncover the emotional truth we're searching for. "Fiction demands that we dive headfirst into puddles of conflict others might choose to sidestep," wrote freelance editor and author Kathryn Craft for Writer Unboxed. "It asks that we scratch and dig until we unearth emotional truths, and then find a way to convey them so that a reader we've never met can share the same journey."

In my experience, it's the sharing that provides the greatest reward. I've rarely felt so moved as when the editor who plucked *Loreena's Gift* out of the slush pile discussed the main character with me. Seeing her through his eyes brought me to tears. Here was a reader who understood the very depths I had gone to in chronicling Loreena's story. It was like he'd reached out and applied a salve on a festering wound. It made me feel I was no longer alone in my struggle.

After that encounter, I had a sense of peace toward the big questions I had pursued throughout the novel. They weren't answered definitively. (Big questions rarely are.) But I had made peace with them and was able to move on. "As children, we ask, 'Why?,'" wrote Kimberly D. S. Reiter, PhD, associate professor of history at Stetson University. "All too often, we learn to accept 'because it just is.'"

A writer doesn't have to accept that answer, though. We get to pursue our questions in all their complexity by simply setting out on the next adventure. How fortunate we are.

Do You Write to Find the Truth?

To find out if truth is one of the benefits you gain from writing, mark the following statements using a scale of 0 to 5, with 5 meaning "almost always" and 0 meaning "never."

_____ When I'm wrestling with one of the big questions in life, I often turn to writing.

_____ I can boil down the themes in my stories to big questions like, "Are humans capable of true unselfishness?" or "Does love ever last?" or "Why do bad things happen to good people?"

_____ When I experience difficult traumas in my life, I feel the urge to write.

_____ Writing helps me make sense of life.

_____ Writing brings me inner peace.

Your total score: _____

13 or higher: Finding truth is likely a frequent benefit of writing for you.

13 or lower: Finding truth may not be one of the benefits of writing for you.

∼

What Truth Are You Seeking in Your Writing?

Take a look at the current story you're writing, or choose the one you'd like to delve into more deeply. To discover the truth you (or your main character) may be seeking, ask your main character the following questions:

- What's causing you the most pain right now?
- What could someone tell you that would bring you the most relief?
- What are you hoping to find—or what quandary are you trying to resolve—by the end of this story?
- What do you hope you won't discover by the end of this story?

Then ask your author self: What has working on this story taught me about life so far? What questions (if any) has it answered?

Review your answers to detect the one overriding question that's rising above the rest. Isolating that question will point you in the direction of the truth you're seeking. Then use that question as a compass to guide the rest of your story.

TEN

Writing to Release Secrets

THERE'S a reason why we keep our diaries stowed away in secret places: we can journal about things we can't talk about. The writing process, with its eerie way of making us feel like we're sharing with a friend, allows us to be honest about our feelings. The fact that many journals begin with the salutation "Dear Diary" signifies that each new entry is written to a confidante who's waiting and wanting to hear what we have to say. This friend doesn't interrupt, judge, or dish out useless advice. It has an unlimited attention span, is always there when needed, and can handle the anger, jealousy, and despair we typically hide from our human friends.

I find it interesting that most authors kept diaries when they were young, acting on a desire to express their hidden emotions. Many couldn't share how they truly felt in any other way and came to the page eager to release some of that burden. Others used diary entries to play around with words, experiment with sound and meaning, and see how a page could be manipulated into demonstrating more clearly what the writer was trying to articulate.

It isn't only these private notebooks that contain secret emotions and experiences. They have a way of bleeding into our stories, too. Yes, our secret struggles and shames often show up in our novels, with the characters playing out scenes that hearken back to our own shadowed times, providing a healthy outlet for feelings long-repressed, sometimes for years.

It's Okay to Talk About That Here

What is it that seduces writers to divulge their innermost secrets on the page? Author Patty Somlo, whom I mentioned in chapter 7, was writing a short story collection when she found herself drifting into her difficult childhood.

"Leticia Williams, the main character in the title story," she wrote for Writing and Wellness, "reappears throughout *Hairway to Heaven*. . . . [She] is a recovering alcoholic—and occasional drug abuser—on the way to building a new, much healthier and happy life. I grew up in an alcoholic family, in which both my parents drank. A career Air Force officer, my father was away from us a lot. That left my mother with the task of raising three children mostly on her own, and she wasn't equipped for that."

As Patty followed Letitia's story, she was surprised by where it led her. "Writing *Hairway*, I had a very rough idea about this world that I wanted to portray. At the same time, I let the story take me where it wanted to go. I didn't know ahead of time where the book would lead me. That miraculous part of writing is, I think, the most exciting, and of course healing, part."

Many writers tell similar stories of difficult childhoods. American author Flannery O'Conner has been quoted as saying, "Anyone who has survived his childhood has enough information about life to last him the rest of his days." Scientists have even found data suggesting that children who were exposed to abuse, neglect, or dysfunctional families tend to be more intensely creative.

In one 2018 study, for instance, researchers asked 234 professional dancers, opera singers, actors, directors, and musicians to complete questionnaires about their childhood experiences. The questionnaires assessed the following:

- Emotional, physical, and sexual abuse
- Emotional and physical neglect
- Household dysfunction (e.g., domestic violence, substance abuse, divorce)

Results showed that the artists with more childhood adversity were more likely to:

- Be more fantasy-prone
- Experience more shame and anxiety
- Have gone through more traumatic events

These individuals were also more likely to have intense creative and existential experiences and regard their creative pursuits as a means of coping with and dealing with past and current traumas. Most importantly, they felt their creative activities gave them *greater control* over the difficult aspects of their lives.

We Write the Story, We Call the Shots

Although any art form can offer an avenue of expression, a means of escape, and a mode of transcendence, writing is unique in that it allows the writer to play God. On the page, we can "rewrite" our experiences so they turn out as we might have liked them to in real life.

"My mother never stopped drinking, was depressed and felt hopeless about changing her life," Patty wrote. "The wonderful healing power of writing *Hairway to Heaven* was that I could take the reality of a difficult childhood I couldn't do anything about, rewrite the story, and transform the pain into art."

Sadly, in real life, abusers often get away with it. Monsters at home are seen as saints in public. Suffering may go on for years without relief, as the victims' cries for help go ignored. But on the page, all that can be changed. The writer wields the ultimate weapon—the pen—and with it comes the delicious satisfaction of retribution, revenge, rescue, and the doling out of well-deserved justice.

When I was thirteen years old, my parents began to take in foster children. Many stayed with us only a short time and then left to live with family members like aunts, uncles, and grandparents. Some, however, were returned to the very parents who had been proven abusive; and yet the powers that be were unable to terminate parental rights.

I remember two young girls in particular. They were about four and seven years old, and they seemed like younger sisters to me. I had been raised with three brothers; and though I loved them all, I had always missed having a sister. So I was excited about the change. All of a sudden, there were girls around who wore dresses, liked horses, and enjoyed fantasy stories like I did. I could play games with them and their dolls, introduce them to the animals on the ranch, and enlist their help in baking cookies. For a little while, I got to experience what it was like to have other girls in the house.

Unfortunately, the sisters had been horribly traumatized. They arrived at our house dirty and barefoot, their faces pale with worry. They had been exposed to sexual abuse—to the point of being filmed without clothes and in sexually suggestive poses by their parents, of all people. Our family knew about their traumas, so we showed the appropriate patience when it came to the girls' bed-wetting and nightmares. Over the time the sisters were with us, as they were exposed to a much more stable family atmosphere, they started to recover and act like normal little girls again. I grew quite attached to them.

Then came the day we got the awful news: The state was sending the girls back to their parents, and there was nothing we could do about it.

I'll never forget the day the caseworker took them away. I had come up against injustices before in my life, but this was one of the worst, and it bothered me for years. So it was no surprise that when I wrote my novel *Loreena's Gift*, I felt a deep sense of satisfaction when some of the nasty characters in the book got their due. It made for some dark scenes, but that was okay with me. In *my story*, the monsters weren't going to get away with it.

"I lived around the corner from a methadone clinic," Patty wrote for Writing and Wellness, "and the bus I took downtown every day to work stopped there, to pick up clients and drop them off. We had a lot of drug dealing and many homeless people on the streets in our neighborhood, including a small group of Native Americans who sat on the stoop across from my house, smoking and drinking all day.

"Just as I couldn't change my childhood, I couldn't alter the reality of these folks' lives, which depressed me. But in *Hairway*, I could reimagine their stories being a bit different. And that made me feel better."

Writing to Make Sense of Experiences

When we're young, we don't have the emotional maturity to fully grasp the things that happen to us. A child who's being bullied in school knows that it feels awful, that he is afraid of the bully, and that he doesn't want to face him again. What he's unlikely to understand is why the bully is the way he is, what motivations might be behind his behavior, and what techniques will best solve the problem.

The same can happen to children growing up in households with alcohol or drug abuse. Instead of understanding the substance's effect on Mom or Dad, the child is more likely to fear the parent's outbursts have something to do with the child's behavior. It's only with maturity that we can look back on traumatic experiences and try to make sense of them.

Author Linda Sienkiewicz didn't realize she was doing just that when she wrote her novel, *In the Context of Love*. She had seen a magazine article titled "My Father Was a Rapist," which was about several young women whose lives were changed when they learned they were conceived in rape. "Their strength, courage and resilience impressed me," she wrote for Writing and Wellness. "Years later, I was looking for a storyline when I remembered the article."

Linda proceeded with the novel, creating the main character, experimenting with point of view, and changing the order of the scenes until she had it just as she wanted it. It wasn't until much later that she realized where the story really came from.

"The novel is about the need for women to tell their stories without shame," she wrote. "The more I developed this story, the more important that theme became. The way victims of sexual assault are shamed by society has always disturbed me, but I didn't relate my own experience of date rape to the novel until recently. I'm certain now that was one of the reasons I felt compelled to write this novel. For years I felt I was to blame for what happened to me, and was sure no one would believe otherwise. Being able to say, at last, 'This happened, it wasn't right, and it hurt me,' was incredibly empowering. Likewise, for the characters in *In the Context of Love*, speaking out is powerful and healing."

Indeed, it seems the things we can't talk about have an almost supernatural way of making it onto the page. My upcoming novel, *The Beached Ones*, includes instances where characters die by suicide. It didn't take too much detective work to realize that my adoptive father's suicide, which occurred when I was very young, was playing out in the shadows of some of the scenes. As I worked my way through the character's story, my own swam up from my unconscious mind to plop itself front and center in my brain, where it demanded answers.

It wasn't until after my mom read the story that I gathered enough courage to ask the questions that had plagued me for years. What happened? How did it happen? I had dim memories from my childhood, but none of them made sense. I needed a death certificate, police report, newspaper articles—something to connect my blurred memories to reality. My mom was kind enough to do some research and get copies of several articles about the incident from the local paper. Finally, I had some concrete details to which I could anchor this difficult experience. With my main character as the catalyst, I managed to find peace and move on.

For author Mary Avery Kabrich, dyslexia was the secret shame she never talked about. She always knew she wanted to be a writer, but her teacher told her in grade school that if she couldn't read, she couldn't write, so she buried the desire. Many years later, after becoming a successful school psychologist, Mary finally returned to that dark, shameful place. Therapy helped her heal her relationship with who she was and allowed her dream of being a writer to surface. "Upon leaving therapy I knew I needed to give voice to this child I had long ago buried," she wrote for Writing and Wellness. "Writing *Once Upon a Time a Sparrow* gave me the opportunity to tell my story with the positive outcome I never dreamed would be possible. . . . Not only did I publicly come out as being dyslexic, but writing this story freed me up to move on and claim myself as a writer."

A Story Doesn't Have to Be a Bestseller to Be Worth It

It's obvious from the many stories recounted here that writing—specifically the act of storytelling—can be transformative. Taking the germ of an experience and turning it into a story others may want to read requires a mental and emotional process that creates its own deeply felt rewards.

Any writer will tell you how awesome it is to hear that a story touched a reader or the reader related to the characters. It's extremely gratifying and has nothing to do with whether the book was a bestseller (or even close). The rewards are there in the writing alone and are compounded with every reader who finds value in the story.

Writing releases us from the ghosts that haunt us. It gives us a way to bring those things we don't talk about into the light, where we can deal with them more objectively and without judgment or censor.

As Truman Capote said, "You can't blame a writer for what the characters say."

Do You Write to Release Your Secrets?

To find out if releasing old traumas or secrets is one of the benefits you gain from writing, answer the following questions using a scale of 0 to 5, with 5 meaning "almost always" and 0 meaning "never."

_____ Many of my characters have similar experiences to those I had in the past.

____ I've been able to process difficult experiences through my stories.

____ Writing about difficult topics I can't talk about has brought me peace.

____ I often feel the blank page is the only place where I can be truly honest.

____ At least one of my stories has allowed me to be more upfront about who I am.

Your total score: ____

13 or higher: Releasing old traumas or secrets is likely a frequent benefit of writing for you.

13 or lower: Releasing old traumas or secrets may not be one of the benefits of writing for you.

Are There Secrets Waiting to Be Told in Your Story?

Sometimes our secrets are hidden even from ourselves. To unearth a secret you may be ready to tell, try the following exercise. The result might form the basis for your next story.

1. **Create a character who's completely different from you.** If

you're shy and reserved, create a character who is outgoing and sassy. If you're popular and well-liked, have your character be a loner. Decide who your character is, imagine them in your head, give them a name if you like, and then move on to step two.

2. **Imagine that this character is struggling with a secret.** You don't have to know what it is yet. Instead, imagine that your character is troubled and that they respond to that inner turmoil by taking a life-changing action. Make it something big, like burning down a building, robbing a place of business, or driving off to Alaska in a broken-down Chevy. In other words, have them do something you would never do. Choose the action, think about it in your head, and then go on to the next step.

3. **Set a timer for twenty minutes, then write the scene.** Let your imagination go so you can write the scene where the character takes this life-changing action. As you write, keep asking yourself, "Why are they doing this? What is bothering them so much that they're willing to take this drastic step?" Keep writing. Don't censor yourself. Let your fingers fly free, and see what comes up. It could be that something is lingering in your subconscious that wants to come out—and that would make a great story.

ELEVEN

Writing to Boost Brainpower

AMERICAN HISTORIAN and author David McCullough once said in an interview, "Writing is thinking. To write well is to think clearly. That's why it's so hard."

Writing is one of the truest reflections of how we think. So when we're thinking clearly, it's likely to transfer to the page. Conversely, if our thoughts are jumbled, unorganized, or not fully formed, that will show through, too.

The magical thing about writing is that the more we practice it, the better thinkers we become. Indeed, writing exercises our thinking muscles so that as the writing improves, so does the thinking, until we notice the beneficial effects even outside of our writing projects and in our everyday lives.

Studies Show that Writing Improves Critical Thinking

How writing affects thinking is such an intriguing topic that scientists have explored it many times over the years. In a 2007 study, Ian J. Quitadamo and colleagues compared the critical thinking performance of two groups of students. They told the first group that their performance in the laboratory portion of their biology class would be evaluated based on their essays instead of the traditional quizzes. Then they told the second group (the control group) that their performance would be evaluated based on the quizzes as usual.

The results showed that critical thinking performance was significantly different between the writing and nonwriting groups. While the writing group showed an increase in critical thinking scores, the nonwriting group showed a *decrease*. In fact, critical thinking improvement in the writing group was approximately *nine times greater* than in the nonwriting group.

The researchers also noticed significant differences in analysis and inference skills. The writing group achieved analysis scores that were fifteen times higher and inference scores that were eight times higher than those from the nonwriting group. A comparison of the essays indicated that writing students improved 53.3 percent over the seven weeks of the study.

"Results indicated that students from the writing group significantly outperformed their nonwriting peers in both total critical thinking skill and the component critical thinking skills of analysis and inference," the researchers wrote. They added that writing demanded more of the students: "It also seems likely that writing students experienced a greater cognitive demand than nonwriting students simply because the writing act required them to hypothesize, debate, and persuade . . . rather than memorize as was the case in nonwriting control courses."

The researchers suggested several reasons why writing had such a powerful effect:

- Writing requires you to clarify your ideas and find ways to effectively communicate them.
- Writing provides an opportunity to think through arguments, cultivating and enabling higher-order thinking.
- Writing can be used as a means to restructure knowledge.
- Writing promotes reflection, which contributes to learning.

This reminds me of a study book I read in college. My older brother handed it down to me, and it sat in my drawer for months, untouched. When some of my classes proved challenging, however, I pulled it out and read through the suggestions. The one that stuck with me advised me to "write notes in your own words." I was an avid notetaker and had been diligently recording the important points my professors made. Then I would review those notes in preparation for the tests.

The book, however, suggested that instead of writing down verbatim what the professor said, I should translate the point into my own words. If this proved impossible during class because of the speed at which the professor moved from one concept to the next, the notes could be written at a later time.

I followed this advice and was amazed at the difference it made. Suddenly I could remember the concepts more easily; and when midterms and finals rolled around, reviewing my interpretations ensured that I did well on the tests.

I am such a believer in this process that, to this day, I recommend that writers who attend my workshops take notes by hand. Technology gives us faster and easier ways to record information, and it's common to see attendees snapping pictures of slides and typing notes on their laptops. But these methods aren't nearly as effective when trying to grasp new concepts. To truly learn what we're being taught, there's no better way than to write the concepts down by hand in our own words. Through writing, our thinking naturally improves.

Writing Helps Us Remember What We Learn

Thinking is hard work. Unfortunately, it's not always taught well in school. Too often students are tasked with simply memorizing and regurgitating facts—which, as we know, are forgotten as soon as the test is over. Writing, on the other hand, etches that knowledge into the brain.

I remember a history assignment from high school. Every semester, our teacher allowed a select number of students to choose a subject, thoroughly research it, and then write a report that would have a major influence on the final grade. We were given a deadline and allowed to spend class time researching. I was thrilled with this assignment and eagerly devoured books upon books about Woodrow Wilson, my chosen subject. As I gathered information and wrote about the twenty-eighth president of the United States, I learned so much and I remember more about him to this day than any other US president in history.

"Students have always struggled with critical thinking that is both difficult to teach and difficult to learn," wrote Josh Carlyle on the blog for the American Board for the Certification of Teacher Excellence. "Students who cannot think critically have a hard time developing their ideas in writing. Teaching students to develop an original idea and support it is more complicated than teaching them how to avoid spelling errors. Critical thinking involves evaluation, problem-solving, and decision making which are all necessary ingredients in a good essay."

Carlyle goes on to state that essay writing improves critical thinking in these ways:

- It requires us to evaluate the reliability of the information at hand.
- It teaches us that facts are provable truths, whereas opinions are based on personal experiences, feelings, and untested beliefs.
- It allows us to understand how we react to information. For example, do we agree or disagree? Does it spark an emotional reaction?
- It requires us to make decisions as to what information to use, how to present it, and how to best argue a position.
- It requires us to solve the problems that are always inherent in writing: how to start the essay, how to organize the middle, and how to end it.
- It encourages us to evaluate existing arguments and potentially find flaws and/or improve them.
- It teaches us how to present arguments in an understandable and persuasive way.

Perhaps best of all, writing about a subject brings us closer to that subject in a way no other method does. There's a reason journalists, magazine writers, and freelance writers make great contestants on the trivia game show *Jeopardy*. They research and write about a lot of topics, and that helps them remember details they can then access as needed to answer various trivia questions.

Indeed, writing improves critical thinking, encourages learning, and helps us retain what we learn. Writing and thinking are so intertwined that, in essence, writing *is* thinking.

Writing Is Thinking

"I believe that one of the reasons students have a difficult time writing is that they spend so much time thinking about what to write before they write as opposed to simply writing what they think; the writing facilitates their thinking—their writing is thinking."

This quote by Neil Haave, an associate professor of biology at the University of Alberta, is from *The National Teaching and Learning Forum*. Haave noted that he attended a conference in 2003 in which he heard a presenter assert that writing is thinking. Until that point, Haave had always thought of writing as simply conveying an idea or information to another person: "a means of transmitting or recording an argument." Upon further reflection, he realized the truth in the statement. "My understanding of writing as thinking has since become further embedded in me, strengthened by the results of daily (well . . . that is my goal at least) writing and also the practice of free-writing by students in class."

Haave had a habit of giving his students regular reading assignments and then asking them to write and report about what they read. He discovered that their one- to two-page typed responses were often filled with complaints about the assignments being too difficult. Initially, he interpreted these complaints as being related to the amount of writing required, but eventually, he realized that the students were really complaining about the difficulty they had in understanding the assigned readings. "If writing is thinking and the writing is difficult, then that means that they are being cognitively challenged," he wrote.

In his paper, "Writing as Thinking," Australian researcher Richard Menary argued that writing required the brain to combine thought processes with the physical act of writing, thereby integrating different sections of the brain to restructure thought. Indeed, we don't simply write sentences, but rather manipulate them to better reflect what we're thinking. This act of manipulation produces other thoughts and ideas so that one task feeds the other in a continual cycle—stimulating certain sections of the brain to work with each other until a new process is born.

So writing is not simply the act of recording what we think. It is much more involved than that, incorporating several different actions by which we clarify and massage our thoughts until one begins to flow into the other. It is at this point when many writers experience the true magic of writing, when a new idea sparks or a new character appears on the scene. Suddenly we see things in the story or article more clearly, all because we engaged in the glorious process of writing.

Writing Stories Improves Thinking

Just as essay and article writing helps us become better thinkers, so does storytelling. A group of scientists, led by Martin Lotze of the University of Greifswald in Germany, used MRI scanners to observe the brains of both experienced and novice writers as they worked on their stories. They first asked the participants to simply copy an excerpt, then to brainstorm and write a short story.

The results showed a significant difference between merely copying and true creative activity. When the participants brainstormed, areas of the brain associated with visualization became more active, indicating the subjects were "seeing" the scenes in their minds. When they started writing, the hippocampus (which is mainly responsible for memory) also became active, perhaps indicating the writer was pulling from known information to inform the evolving story. A third section of the brain that was responsible for holding several pieces of information at once lit up as well, possibly indicating the writer was juggling plot lines and/or characters. These areas were not active when the participants simply copied the excerpt.

In essence, the experiment showed that writing or plotting a story stimulated areas of the brain to come to life in new ways—so clearly that neuroscientists could see from an MRI image whether the subject was actively writing.

What is even more interesting is that the researchers found a significant difference between amateur and expert writers. During brainstorming sessions, the experts' brains showed more activity in the speech/language regions than in the visualization centers, suggesting a different strategy in storytelling. Researchers speculated that while the amateur writers were "seeing" the story like a film in their heads, the more experienced writers were listening to an inner narrative voice. There were also other differences once the participants started to write. In the experienced writers, a deep area of the brain called the caudate became active. With the amateurs, however, the caudate remained quiet.

Whenever we learn a new skill like driving, we have to concentrate intensely on every little action, from pushing the gas pedal and checking the rearview mirror to steering and watching for road signs. As we gain skill, these activities become automatic, and the caudate takes over. It seems this is what occurred in the brains of the more experienced writers in Lotze and colleagues' study. As they gained skill, they naturally combined many activities involved in writing into a series of automatic responses, indicating a certain level of mastery.

The researchers also compared the creativity between the two groups and found that the more experienced writers scored higher on verbal creativity tests and written creativity evaluations. The scientists felt this surely reflected the different connectivity seen in the brains of the experienced writers compared to the amateurs.

This is exciting because it suggests we can *boost our brainpower the more we write.* Sticking to a regular writing practice and continually honing our craft can change our brains over time, creating more connections among the various regions until we become more adept at not only storytelling but overall creativity as well.

So effective is creative writing at improving our brainpower that some professors wish it received more emphasis in school. Patrick T. Randolph, an independent researcher and professor at Western Michigan University, suggested in his paper, "Using Creative Writing as a Bridge to Enhance Academic Writing," that teachers pay more attention to the benefits of creative writing, as opposed to research papers and other standard types of academic writing.

"Academic writing," he wrote, "with its formulaic style, is both rigid and limiting. However, with creative writing, students learn a number of ways to communicate their thoughts, and, at the same time, express their own originality in different forms of writing: poetry, short stories, creative letters, essays, peer reviews, and formal critiques. Therefore, creative writing, based on neuro research, is actually 'healthier' than academic writing."

Writing Inspires Mental Changes

The great science fiction writer Ray Bradbury is quoted as saying, "Writing is ninety-nine percent thinking, and the rest is typing." Because writing is such a mentally demanding task, writers often have difficulty doing it on days they feel fatigued. I know that after several hours of writing, even though I have only been standing or sitting at the computer, I have to take a break—often a short power nap—to recover. My daily routine consists of working on my novel first thing in the morning, then four to five hours on freelance projects, followed by a nap. The nap helps refresh and prime my brain for more writing in the evening, which may include blog posts, course material, and nonfiction books like this one. Without that nap, my brain simply won't cooperate.

Because I've regularly pushed myself to write more, today I can accomplish multiple forms of writing encompassing thousands of words in a single day, and yet I feel ready to do it all over again the next day. (Until the weekend, of course. That's when my brain crashes!) Writing is never really easy, but it's become automatic to the point that I can continue for longer periods before needing a break.

Perhaps most rewarding, though, are the changes I've noticed in my thinking. As the studies discussed in this chapter suggest, there's no doubt that writing keeps my thinking sharp. I only hope it continues as I get older, for the mental play that goes on when writing a story is a source of joy I'd hate to lose. If you feel the same way, you're enjoying one of the many gifts of writing—increased brainpower—which is a powerful reason why your writing matters.

Does Writing Boost Your Brainpower?

To find out if increased brainpower is one of the benefits you gain from writing, answer the following questions using a scale of 0 to 5, with 5 meaning "almost always" and 0 meaning "never."

_____ Writing makes my brain more responsive and creative.
_____ Writing has given me a better understanding of human nature.
_____ My writing has taught me so much.
_____ My newer stories are more complex and accomplished than my earlier ones.
_____ I think I'm an adept conversationalist.
_____ I feel confident in my ability to grasp difficult concepts.

Your total score: _____

13 or higher: Your writing is most likely increasing your brainpower.
13 or lower: It may be early in your writing career, but keep writing and improving your skills. You may see a change in the future.

Let Your Writing Challenge Your Brain

To get to know your characters better and to challenge your brain, try the following exercise.

1. Pick two characters who are already in your story, or create two new characters and give them names. Write their names next to each other at the top of the page.
2. Under each name, list the following for each character: age, marital status, education level, job, place of residence, economic level, hobbies, typical clothing, and basic notes about appearance.
3. Choose a current debatable issue (marijuana legalization, global warming, capital punishment, etc.), and write three to four paragraphs on that issue from each character's point of view. Do your best to represent your character's true personality and thinking process.
4. Write three to four paragraphs on the same issue from your own point of view.
5. Read over the three samples, and observe the differences.

TWELVE

Writing to Know Your True Self

HOW WELL YOU know your true self can determine the quality of your life. Many of us spend precious little time, however, discovering who we really are. We rarely pause for reflection on the topic as we hurry through our education to arrive at an occupation; and though we may take a personality test here and there or ask friends for insights, we tend to proceed on autopilot while hoping for the best.

If you want to live a truly authentic life, however—one that allows you to reach your full potential and engage your strengths toward a higher purpose—you must get clear about who you are, what you want, and what your priorities are in life. Fortunately, if you're a writer, you have a built-in process to help you do just that.

Other Authors Give Us Insights into Ourselves

The first time I saw author Andre Dubus III, I was at a writing conference in Florida. In preparation for the event, I had read his novel *The Garden of Last Days,* along with several other novels written by the other author instructors and presenters. It was actually my mom's idea to do this. She attended the conference with me (she didn't go to the classes but went to the free readings every night) and wanted to know the authors' work before hearing them speak. So she and I compared notes about the books; and although our tastes differ, we both appreciate good writing. Mom was most looking forward to Ann Patchett's reading and interview. I was eager to see Andre Dubus III. His book was my favorite. I was taken by its depth of characterization and rawness of emotion and had felt uniquely drawn into the story.

There's a truth that exists in life that can be extremely helpful to us if we embrace it: What we admire in others, we also have in ourselves. This means that although we can objectively notice the talents of others, we don't usually feel a connection with them or a deep admiration for them unless we see something in them that resonates deep within us.

As clinical psychologist John Gressel, PhD, wrote for *Psychology Today* online, "Take a moment and think about someone you admire more than anyone else in your life: what is it about this man or woman that makes you look up to him or her? Really try to hone in on the one or two qualities of the person you admire. Now hear this: those qualities are in you, seeking to come out, and that's why you're able to see them so clearly in another person."

Success coach and author Gail Thackray agrees with this. "You can only recognize the traits in someone else that you possess yourself or you wouldn't be able to recognize it," she wrote on her blog. "You may think that everyone must admire that person for that trait, but you would be very surprised to find out otherwise."

Perhaps nowhere did this truth show itself more clearly to me than at that conference in Florida. When the other authors talked about their writing processes, they praised outlining, planning, and plotting, explaining all the ways they thought through their stories before even beginning to stitch together the actual scenes. These award-winning literary authors stood high on their pedestals (in my mind) and spoke of story blueprints I knew I could never imitate. I'd tried their methods before and failed miserably. After having a go at outlining a novel, I quickly lost interest and never tried it again.

I listened to them talk about structure, rules, guidelines, and genres; and though I remained open to anything I might learn, I felt disconnected and doubtful I'd become the writer I wished to be, as I couldn't duplicate what they were suggesting.

Then it came time for Andre Dubus III's interview. As he spoke about his writing process and how he had come to writing in the first place, everything changed for me. It turned out that my favorite author at the conference had a writing process—indeed, an entire approach and feel for writing—that was completely akin to mine. I felt like he had taken the unformed thoughts in my head and put them into words that described perfectly how I felt. He was speaking my language when none of the others were.

Andre eschewed outlining. It made the writing stilted and predictable, he said (I'm writing this from memory), and limited the creative process. It also put the author's ego too powerfully into the story. Just go with your character and write, he advised. Dive underwater to that place where your imagination lives, and see where it takes you.

I've never felt so completely validated. If this amazing, award-winning giant of an author could speak about writing in ways that described how I felt about it even better than I could, then certainly my approach couldn't be so off-base. That meant there was hope I could still become a good writer. Perhaps more importantly, it also meant that my creative process wasn't "wrong." In fact, it might be more right than all the other methods of writing I'd been hearing about—at least for me. At that moment, I felt Andre had given me the gift of myself, and I've never forgotten it.

Writing Brings You Closer to Your True Self

I've made this chapter the last one in this section because, of all the benefits writing has to give us, I think the most precious is the gift of getting to know our true selves. Somehow, through our regular writing practice, we not only learn about who we are but also how to accept and honor ourselves—something many of us struggle with before writing finds us.

Andre Dubus III describes in his memoir, *Townie*, the first time he sat down to write. He had grown up in a tough neighborhood with a single mom and often keenly felt the responsibility of protecting his family. (His father, the celebrated short story author Andre Dubus, moved out when Andre was young.) He had to toughen up early, which meant his more sensitive nature was often repressed. After surviving frequent violent situations, he developed into an angry young man who could fly off the handle at the slightest provocation. On the day he finally sat down and put pen to paper, something changed.

"I felt more like me than I ever had," he wrote in *Townie*, "as if the years I'd lived so far had formed layers of skin and muscle over myself that others saw as me when the real one had been underneath all along, and writing—even writing badly—had peeled away those layers, and I knew then that if I wanted to stay this awake and alive, if I wanted to stay me, I would have to keep writing."

If I wanted to stay me, I would have to keep writing. Those are words many writers can relate to.

Who Am I, Really?

We're often told that if we want to get to know ourselves, we need to explore our values, interests, strengths, and passions. List those things you enjoy—and voila! There you are. List those things that are important to you, and your true self will be revealed. List your strengths, and you'll find your purpose. Determine what you're passionate about, and discover the source of your energy.

These are all important things to consider. But in my experience, going through exercises such as these doesn't end the search for your true self. You may have heard the suggestion to examine the most meaningful events in your life. Do that carefully, and you can gather more insight into who you are and where you'd like to go. Some also advocate for trying new things. Go bungee jumping, for example, and you may find that you're braver than you realized, that you enjoy adventure, or that you fear heights and never want to go bungee jumping again. Take a trip to the ocean, and you may feel like the water is an integral part of you or that you far prefer a peaceful mountain lake. Sign up for a cooking class, and you may discover a hidden talent for the culinary arts or realize you'd rather avoid the kitchen for the rest of your life.

Journaling and Freewriting to Find Your True Self

Indeed, many exercises can help us chip away at this inner being we call the "self," but none are as effective as writing. Even therapists recommend journaling for this very purpose. Manhattan Mental Health Counseling, for instance, offers five journaling exercises to get to know yourself a lot better in one of their blog posts. "Regular journaling can be a powerful tool to generate better self-awareness," they note on their website. "By putting your thoughts on paper regularly, you can process feelings, trigger memories and unlock motivations you didn't realize you had."

They suggest freewriting, the practice of simply writing for a set period of time without stopping, ignoring grammar and spelling to enable the thoughts to flow. Other ideas include the following:

- Writing about a photograph
- Composing a letter you'll never send (to yourself, a friend, someone in your past, or someone else significant in your life)
- Creating "sentence starters" that encourage reflection, such as "If I could visit my five-year-old self, I'd tell him/her . . ."

Margarita Tartakovsky, MS, writing for *PsychCentral*, states that journaling is one of the most powerful ways to get to know yourself, helping connect you to your inner wisdom. She quotes Sandy Grason, author of the book *Journalution: Journaling to Awaken Your Inner Voice, Heal Your Life and Manifest Your Dreams,* who wrote, "I believe each time you give yourself fully to the blank page, you get a little bit closer to your true Self. It's the place that your greatness can whisper to you and remind you of all that you came to this earth to be."

I have found journaling to be a window into my ability to see the truth in myself and those around me. When I review journal entries from years past, the one thing that most surprises me is how often I have been right about people, events, and the best choices for my future. I have noticed characteristics on a first date, for instance, that turned out to be the very ones that made the relationship unsustainable. If I had only trusted myself more completely, I could have saved myself months of pain and conflict. In rereading my journals, I have learned to trust my instincts more thoroughly.

Writing gives us this gift of insight into our true selves. Writing stories helps us go even further.

The Excavation and Life-Building Art of Writing Stories

There's a reason the word *journey* is used so frequently to describe the writing life. It's the perfect word to illustrate how we move from idea to first draft, from editing to publishing, from publishing to marketing, and from book to book. But the journey is also one of coming to know ourselves better through our story writing.

"Rereading my old stories gives me a snapshot of who I was and what was important to me at the time I wrote those books," wrote author Julie C. Dao for *PubCrawl*. She suggests looking back at your own stories to find common elements and themes to gain new insights into your psyche. I have done this and found that certain themes tend to appear again and again. These themes are important to me, or else they wouldn't keep showing up. This is one of the benefits of writing many books: you gather data and evidence that gives you clues about yourself. I'm not saying that your books are direct windows into your personality. I tend to get irritated when people try to find me in my characters, for instance, as if writers cannot write about those who are different from themselves. Nevertheless, our books are our creations, and they can often reveal through theme and metaphor—and yes, sometimes even more directly through a character or scene—visions that mirror our true selves.

We don't tend to recognize these clues at first. It takes time and reflection and amassing thousands of pages helps. I can say from experience that once you discover the secrets hidden in your stories that reveal your true self, they can bring you not only a sense of peace and knowing, but also a way to improve your work. I've gotten to the point now where I seek out the themes I know are bound to be there. Once I find them, I can use them to make the story stronger and increase my involvement with the characters, which naturally infuses more life into my words.

American author Willa Cather was quoted as saying, "[A] creative writer can do his best only with what lies within the range and character of his deepest sympathies." Yet we must know what those sympathies are to focus our writing practice and have a shot at reaching our greatest potential. All the simple exercises in the world are unlikely to dig deep enough to unearth this type of self-knowledge. Writing stories may be one of the few methods of true self-discovery we have available to us.

Spending Time with Our Characters Improves Self-Compassion

One of the amazing things about writing is that the writer must *be* each character in turn, much as an actor lives in character when taking on a role to accurately portray that person in a movie or TV show. When we do this, we learn what it's like to see life from that character's point of view, instilling within us compassion not only for the character but also for the facets of their personality that may reflect aspects of our own.

This idea of spending time in another character's shoes is so effective in creating both self- and other-compassion that scientists recommend physicians read fiction. ENT (head and neck) surgeon and author Gabriel Weston—who actually got a degree in English literature before going into medicine—wrote an article for the scientific journal *The Lancet* about how reading literature helps a physician develop empathy.

Weston was twenty-four years old when she realized that medicine was her calling, and she was afraid her English lit degree had been a waste of time. Later, she realized how wrong she was. In her *Lancet* article, she tells the story of when she was a junior doctor at an emergency department and how a man came in "whom none of us doctors wanted to see." He was old, cursing, smelling of liquor, and covered in blood.

"What would we learn from someone like this?" Weston wrote. "He was drunk and messy and would probably be verbally abusive."

Somehow, Weston ended up treating the man. While helping to clean the blood off him, she learned that he had been a lawyer, that his son had died of a heroin overdose, and that his wife had left him after their son's death. So he started drinking and lost his job and his house, eventually ending up on the streets. That night, he had been attacked by a group of young men.

Weston realized as the old man talked that she had horribly misjudged him: "What had I assumed when I first saw him coming into the department that evening, painted with blood? That he was a loser, someone worthless? What kind of doctor was I to have written him off in this way?"

She then wrote that she should have known better, not only because she was older than her peers, but also because of her degree in English lit: "I thought of Magwitch, Charles Dickens' munificent convict in the marshes, I thought of Macbeth and Medea committing their crimes of regicide and child-killing. I thought of the eponymous protagonist in Lionel Shriver's *We Need to Talk About Kevin* which I had just finished reading. None of the great characters in literature were clean or simple or saccharine-coated. People were more interesting than that, and more difficult."

Weston went on to say that she thinks of that night often, and of how literature and doctoring go together. Reading literature, she says, "forces one to listen to people in a different way," a more open and accepting way. This type of listening not only helps a doctor better understand what a patient may be going through, but also can "fall on the patient like a kind of balm."

Imagine then, how much more beneficial writing must be in helping us to develop compassion not only for others but for ourselves. We can't do one without automatically doing the other. Compassion is a characteristic that applies universally and doesn't discriminate. As we become intimately familiar with our characters, the heroes and villains, the strange and the delightful, we have the opportunity to grow in our compassion even more than readers do—and to emerge reformed.

Why "Knowing Oneself" Matters

Perhaps all this sounds familiar to you, and you agree that writing helps you get to know yourself. But is that such an important benefit?

According to research, the better you know yourself, the happier you'll be. Improving self-awareness can help you make better life decisions, for one. The better you know yourself, the more likely you are to set goals that fit with your life's purpose and to go after them with high energy and motivation. This, in turn, gives your days a sense of meaning that they often lack if you don't understand yourself. We often hear the phrase "Be true to yourself," but this is not possible if you don't know the person to whom you're supposed to be true.

"Self-awareness or knowing oneself is one of the cornerstones for happiness and success in life," wrote life coach Tomas Svitorka. "Without good awareness, people often pursue the wrong career (usually because it pays well or it's easy to do), get in a relationship with the wrong person, struggle with indecisiveness and low self-confidence, and generally find themselves just going along with things."

Knowing yourself is also a prerequisite to achieving true success. With this knowledge, you can better manage your business and personal relationships. Researchers reported in 2017 that when participants went through a training course to help them get to know themselves better, they improved their "social intelligence," or their ability to understand others' feelings, intentions, and beliefs.

Knowing yourself makes it easier to seek out others who share your passions and interests, choose occupations that better suit your temperament, and even find more joy in your leisure time. It also provides a natural resistance to envy and protects you from the modern-day malaise that comes with comparing yourself with others on social media. Being clear about who you are, what you want, and where you're going acts like a shield against the feeling that you "should do" what others are doing to be successful.

You may agree that knowing yourself is a good thing and believe you're doing pretty well at it, but then have the nagging feeling that the person in the mirror is still a mystery in many ways. Pause for a minute to ask yourself what you really want before you die, and you may have a hard time answering. Ask why you feel or behave the way you do at certain times, and you may struggle to come up with anything satisfying. Ask why you tend to be attracted to certain characters in your stories or real life, and all you may imagine is a big question mark. Indeed, it's very common to have some ideas about who we are but to also find that our understanding of our true selves is rather patchy and inconsistent.

Nowhere are we more alone than when writing our stories; and for many of us, existing in that lonely place day in and day out while adhering to our writing practices is perhaps the greatest challenge of being a writer. But as we gain the discipline needed to sink into our imaginary worlds time and time again, we are rewarded with the gift of truly knowing our characters, who, in turn, help us discover and reflect on the various facets of our inner selves. With them, we seek the treasure that is our uniqueness, while allowing them to assist us in showing compassion to our true selves, thereby achieving a happier existence.

There's no greater gift that writing can give us.

Does Writing Help You Get to Know Yourself?

To find out if self-knowledge is one of the benefits you gain from writing, answer the following questions using a scale of 0 to 5, with 5 meaning "almost always" and 0 meaning "never."

_____ I have learned more about myself through my writing.

_____ Some (or perhaps many) of my characters share my traits;

and when I write from their points of view, I feel more compassion toward myself.

_____ I feel a greater sense of self-acceptance after writing a book.

_____ I feel more myself when writing than while doing most other activities.

_____ I believe that writing has helped me become a better person.

Your total score: _____

13 or higher: Your writing is most likely helping you learn more about your true self.

13 or lower: You might not notice any insights into your true self yet, but keep writing and you'll likely experience growth in this area.

Learn More About Your True Self

To learn more about your true self, you only need to review your body of work to examine how your themes and characters mirror what exists within you. Think of all the stories you've written so far, then answer the following questions:

- What main themes tend to show up in different stories? Do any occur more than once—or even multiple times? If so, take a closer look throughout your work to see how these themes apply to your life.
- What types of characters do you mostly write about? What parts of your personality do they reflect?
- What ideas have you explored in your writing? What is their importance in your daily life?

Make the Big Decision

"Making a decision to write was a lot like deciding to jump into a frozen lake."

~Maya Angelou

THIRTEEN

When Writing is Not the Best Choice

THE PREVIOUS SECTION just laid out in detail the six significant ways writing could benefit your life. It's likely you recognized one or more of those benefits as applicable to you and your writing practice. If so, you've found at least one reason why writing matters to you and is an integral part of your life even if it doesn't make you rich or famous.

If you didn't relate to any of these benefits, however, you're probably wondering if you should continue to invest time and effort into writing. Or perhaps you fell into the category that agrees that writing provides some benefits, but you're still not sure you want to pursue (or continue to pursue) being a writer.

Though I'm a firm believer that writing is good for everyone, I also understand that there are only so many hours in the day and precious few available to devote to valued activities. If you're thinking that you may be better off pouring your passions into something else, or if you doubt writing has a place in your life, this chapter should help you sort things out.

So far, we've reviewed all the reasons to continue writing no matter what outside rewards it may or may not bring. In this chapter, it's time to flip that coin and examine the reasons why you might *not* want to continue writing, or at least cut back on the time and energy you're putting into it.

Seven Reasons Not to Be a Writer

First, we need to define what it means to be a writer. Anyone can keep a journal, write a blog post now and then, or perform writing assignments on the job. To be a writer means you have a desire for writing to occupy a central place in your life and have dreams of being a novelist, short story writer, poet, or nonfiction writer. You may also have a daily writing practice with goals that include publishing your works and building a readership.

Being a writer means seeing writing as part of your identity and laboring over your work in an effort to make it as good as you can. A writer struggles to improve, taking a long-term view of this journey.

Knowing this, let's examine seven reasons why you might *not* want to continue on the path to becoming a writer.

1. You're Looking to Get Rich Quick

If you're thinking of writing as a way to make money, there's nothing wrong with that. But the odds are against you—at least, early on—unless you're a professional who already has a large following that translates into a ready-made readership. Celebrities also fall into this category and frequently experience success when writing especially their memoirs, nonfiction, or children's books.

The key thing here is that these individuals *already have strong platforms* and a fan base interested in any books they write. What's more, they have typically made the bulk of their money elsewhere and are not relying on their books for financial freedom. For the rest of us who imagine writing books as an easy way to make money, publishing is likely to be a disappointment. The market is difficult and only becoming more so. Traditional publishers no longer nurture their authors' careers. Instead, they focus most of their marketing attention (and money) on celebrities and established authors. Sure, one can easily self-publish, but odds are that a profit may be elusive (particularly if you put the proper resources into editing and design), especially early on.

The typical writer, therefore, usually ends up putting more money into publishing a book than he gets back, at least until he builds up an established readership. Even then, book publishing is not a big-money game. If it was, bookstores wouldn't be closing, publishers consolidating, and the majority of authors working full- or part-time jobs to get by.

If you're pursuing writing for money, you're going to travel a rough and frustrating road unless you're open to other more successful ways of reaching your goal. If you're sold on writing, there's freelance writing. Freelancers are hired to write for individuals, businesses, organizations, and entrepreneurs. Payment is guaranteed, making this option a promising way to build a money-making business while taking advantage of your skill and love of writing.

But if you have your heart set on making a full-time living writing books, think again. It's true that some writers succeed, but they're often master marketers. They not only write and produce quality books quickly, but they've also mastered how to market their work consistently enough to create a profit. But even these writers typically have side jobs—at least until they become established—or have partners who help cover the bills.

There are always the exceptions, but don't be fooled. These rags-to-riches stories are very rare, and writing books to get rich quick is generally a losing gamble. If you're looking to get rich, writing is *not* for you.

2. You Want to Be Famous

Let's be honest: all writers want to have their work noticed. We all want to be *seen*. As we discussed in chapter 7, the process of writing helps heal traumas, old wounds, and other emotional difficulties. But don't equate writing with publishing. Writing may heal or fulfill a need, but publishing is a business. It's unrealistic to rely on a business venture to bring you the attention you crave. Here's why.

You never know how your work will be received. And, sadly, quality work goes ignored all the time. Even writers who earn awards often sell low numbers of their prize-winning books, never experiencing the fame they may well deserve. Others who write well often lack the resources to market their work effectively and watch their books languish on websites, ignored.

One thing I've learned over my decades of writing is that there are a *lot* of amazing and talented writers out there—more than you may realize. Writing talent is not reserved for only a very few; talented writers are everywhere. Their work can be found in writing workshops, high schools, local newspapers, MA programs, blog posts, small journals, and on obscure indie publisher's websites. You need not search very far to read something by a talented writer.

But being talented doesn't mean being famous. The market is saturated with books, and it's harder than ever to rise to great notoriety. On top of that, writers are rarely celebrities in today's world. Start naming the famous ones now, and you're likely to run out of names before you raise all ten fingers.

Even the few famous writers we admire today typically developed their fame over long periods of time and are very prolific, with great bodies of work that define them. Expecting you can reach the same level with one or two novels is not only unrealistic, but also a mindset that's sure to leave you disappointed. Even if you are prolific, you may go your whole life with only a small number of readers devoted to you.

For many writers, this is enough. But not becoming famous can be a tough blow, particularly if your greatest desire is to reach celebrity status. If this sounds like you, acknowledge this desire and don't judge yourself. Instead, understand that writing is unlikely to fulfill this desire, and look for other ways to receive the recognition you crave. You may also want to examine your need for attention and see if you can boost your self-esteem and self-worth to the point where your own good opinion of yourself is enough to satisfy you.

3. You Hate Spending Countless Hours Alone with a Laptop

There's no getting around it: serious writers spend hours alone writing. Like any other skill, to do it well, you must practice it daily. Even a few days away from your novel can put you behind, to the extent that it takes you a session or two to get back into the same frame of mind so you can continue the story.

Being a writer is a lot like being an athlete. You won't win the race if you don't train consistently and carefully. Every day you sit down (or stand up!) to write, you're putting in your training time. Just as the marathon runner who trains even on those mornings when she doesn't feel like it, or the gymnast who cancels a week-long cruise to keep his body in shape before the meet, a writer must accept and embrace a life of daily (or near daily) writing, which is, in essence, how writers stay in shape.

I do my best to keep up with a regular fitness program, and I'm always amazed at how weak my muscles get after I take just a week off. Even this short time away means I have to dig in and work hard for a week or two just to get my body back to where it was.

The same is true of writing. Time away dulls the mind and interrupts the daily habit of creating. It takes extra energy and willpower to get back into the groove. Writers who want to succeed must devote themselves to this disciplined approach, returning to the blank page again and again, putting in the time and sharing the space with only themselves, their characters, and their laptops.

This is the part many writers find difficult. They may feel guilty when writing takes time away from family or other important activities, or feel lonely when writing and have to force themselves to do it, as if it were a chore.

Becoming a writer is a mostly solitary endeavor. So if you're not ready to make the sacrifices required, then the writing life is probably not for you.

4. You Prefer to Spend Your Time Daydreaming

Answer this question honestly: When you dream of living the writer's life, does that life include hours of walking blissfully through pastoral scenes with your loyal pup by your side? Do you imagine daydreaming while staring out your picture window at a lake, ocean, or forest until a story idea comes to you? Do you envision writing for an hour or two, then taking a break for a nap or a chef-inspired lunch?

These are delightful fantasies, but that is all they are. We've all read about authors who own cabins, ranch houses, beach houses, and other enticing locations where they can concentrate on their work and not be bothered by the challenges of everyday life. But if you don't already own such a getaway, it's time to wake up to reality.

The real writing life is *nothing like this*. As a modern-day writer, you must work your ass off, if I can be so blunt. In addition to devoting time to a daily writing practice—which is enough of a challenge, since you probably have to work in addition to taking care of your family—you must devote extra hours to marketing and building a platform, making connections with readers, and doing other time-consuming activities to get your work noticed. Every spare moment is typically spent engaged in one of these activities, and it's not like you can do them for a short time and then sit back and enjoy the fruits of your labors. Publishing doesn't work that way. If you build your author platform and start making some money, you can always hire help. But the need for regular writing and marketing never lets up as long as you want to continue to build your writing career.

The writing life is a beautiful one for those who are realistic about what it takes to succeed, but it doesn't resemble the old-fashioned fantasy. To achieve your dream, you'll need to work hard. But if you enjoy what you're doing, you'll love it. If not, you may soon wish you'd made a different choice.

5. You Don't Care What Readers Think

This one is a tough one, as I'm a firm believer that writing for yourself comes first and foremost. But if you want to succeed at building a readership, you need to publish your work at some point, which means caring what readers think of it.

Some writers insist they don't care about readers' opinions, but this is often a defense tactic against a disappointing outcome such as a rejection or lackluster book launch. Of course, if you truly don't care and want to write solely for yourself, then there's no reason to publish. If that's really how you feel, then put your work into a drawer (or on a flash drive) and be happy.

On the other hand, if you want to write *and* be read, learn to write well enough to satisfy readers. The plethora of poorly written self-published books stands as evidence that too many writers haven't embraced or understood this crucial step.

Think back to your childhood. Did you take piano lessons? (Even if you didn't, follow my logic here.) Piano students learn how to read music, count rhythms, hold their hands correctly over the keys, and use different forms of pressure to produce different tones and volumes. They study certain composers to learn the basics of composition and form, then spend hours practicing their pieces and performing them for their teachers for feedback, encouragement, and correction.

This process typically goes on for years, as long as the student doesn't quit. Even then, a piano player may not be considered to have mastered the instrument. Additional training, such as in a college or via a mentoring situation, is often required to become a true "pianist."

Most people understand this. They expect that to play an instrument proficiently, they must learn the fundamentals, practice regularly, gain feedback and guidance from a mentor, keep practicing, and then hopefully, over time, become proficient and perhaps even reach a level of mastery. But when it comes to the art of writing, people think these steps are unnecessary. After all, everyone learned to "write" in school, right?

Unfortunately, writers who operate under this belief are the ones who are left dismally disappointed. It's one thing to learn to write well enough to manage your daily life. It's another to learn the art of storytelling. To be a successful writer with a respectable readership, you must follow a path similar to the one you'd follow to become a pianist, painter, or dancer. You need to learn the fundamentals, practice regularly, and work with a mentor for feedback, encouragement, and correction. Your natural writing talent alone won't make you successful. To get your writing up to the quality readers expect, you need to cultivate and nourish your talent—and pay your dues without complaint. Don't expect the world to hand you a successful writing career on a platter. Expect to work hard for it. Those who enjoy the process are happy to do whatever it takes. If this is you, know that over time, you'll develop the skills necessary to confidently compete with other talented writers. But if this sounds like drudgery, save yourself from the torture.

6. You're Big on Feeling Appreciated

Feeling unappreciated from time to time is a fact of life. Sure, there are those precious moments when a student gives you a handwritten thank-you note or your boss grants you a raise, but these are usually few and far between. It's a shame, because appreciation has a huge impact on employee performance, engagement, and retention.

One study by Clear Review, a performance review software system, found that a lack of appreciation was the number one workplace frustration among employees. Being recognized or appreciated validates the fact that our good work is valued by others and, in turn, makes us feel valued. The simple act of appreciation, when directed our way, makes it more likely we'll work harder and be more dedicated. When we're shown appreciation, satisfaction increases, productivity rises, and we're motivated to improve.

Researchers from the Wharton School at the University of Pennsylvania found this to be true in a study on two groups of people assigned to a fundraising project. The first group was assigned simply to make phone calls to solicit donations. The second group received a pep talk from the director of the project before they started doing the same. In it, the director told the fundraisers how grateful she was for their efforts. During the following week, those who heard the pep talk made 50 percent more fundraising calls than those who didn't.

Feeling appreciated feels good for several reasons. It gives us a sense of connection with others, makes us feel valued, and makes our work seem worth the effort we put into it. Lack of appreciation, on the other hand, decreases energy and motivation, devalues self-worth, and promotes a feeling of isolation. When we find ourselves being unappreciated, our options are limited to the following:

- Taking our talents elsewhere, where they will be appreciated
- Working even harder in the hopes of gaining the appreciation we crave
- Engaging in self-appreciation

Here's the bad news: As a writer, you're unlikely to feel much appreciation for all your hard work, at least until you establish a thriving author platform. Most writers spend years toiling away at their craft with barely a positive word. If you're lucky, you may earn praise from a few early readers. But for quite some time, you have to be willing to endure self-doubt and much questioning about whether your efforts are worthwhile. Choosing to be a writer means striking out on your own with no boss or manager to pat you on the back and no peers to be impressed with your contributions. There is no bonus for overtime hours and no yearly raise. Indeed, the early writing life can instill you with a sense of invisibility.

This isn't necessarily a bad thing. In fact, that early period of writing with little to no appreciation can be an important part of the journey. Today's culture is so centered on celebrity that writers can forget they're actually artists answering their highest calling to create works of art. In the beginning, operating invisibly is the best way to learn, grow, and discover our unique voices while we're still under the radar. Many authors who do reach bestseller status speak of missing that time of writing in obscurity.

Eventually, though, we hope to find readers and become better known. When you reach the point where you're ready to get serious about marketing your work, there are ways to build your platform that are both rewarding and meaningful and will help you feel appreciated. (I refer you to my book, *Writer Get Noticed!*, for more information on how to do that.) But in the beginning—perhaps for several years—prepare to work mostly with little if any appreciation coming your way. If you really need that frequent pat on the back, you may want to search for another path.

7. The Process of Writing Doesn't Make Your Soul Sing

How do you feel after a writing session? This, perhaps more than anything, will tell you whether becoming a writer is the right choice for you.

I have fond memories of my early days of writing novels. Certain writing sessions were so thrilling and unexpected that I couldn't contain myself afterward and had to go leaping around the house just to expel the excited energy. This usually happened after a new character showed up on the scene or something so delicious occurred in the plot that I couldn't believe my good fortune. It was always a surprise of sorts that instilled in me new feelings of awe for the creative process. To this day, I still get butterflies in my stomach when something goes right in a story or when a plot comes together in a way I couldn't foresee.

Of course, it's not always like this. There are plenty of down days when I'm convinced what I'm writing is crap and should be dumped in the trash can. There are months spent banging my head against a wall, trying to figure out where a story is *going*. I have periods of doubt when I question if I have anything of value to offer my readers. But in the end, I love writing for the sake of writing. I love how it feels to begin a new story and the challenge of following it through to the end. I love exploring the big questions, living my characters' lives, traveling to different settings in my mind, and overall indulging my imagination on the page.

After interviewing over 300 writers, I've found that this one thing—the love of writing—is what connects us all. There's just something about it that makes sense to us, and it fills that space inside of us like nothing else can.

Ask yourself if writing affects you this way. If the actual process of writing feels more like a chore than a pleasure, the writing life might not be for you. I'm not saying that writing isn't hard for writers. For most of us, it's the most challenging thing we do. As German novelist Thomas Mann wrote in *Essays of Three Decades*, "A writer is someone for whom writing is more difficult than it is for other people."

For writers, it's the reward that keeps us going. You know it when you feel it—that inner bubbling-up of positive emotions that accompanies a successful writing session. Watch for it. Pay attention to it. Nurture it. It is the *most important influence* in your writing life, for it will sustain you when everything else fails.

When you love the sheer process of writing, you'll make it through the tough times. If you don't, you simply shouldn't torture yourself. Your soul is telling you there is another path for you to follow. Never feel guilty for honoring your feelings. There is no shame in saying, "This just isn't for me." But when you love writing, you owe it to yourself to nurture that positive feeling and see where it takes you.

"Why do you write?" wrote author Crissy Langwell on her blog. "That's what I have to remember every single time I want to throw in the towel. It's not about getting famous or making money. Those would be great side benefits, but that's not why I'm doing this. I write because I love it, because it fills my soul, then allows me to see my soul on the page, and then share my soul with readers. I write because I must, and there's no giving up on that."

Amen.

Dig Deeper into Your Psyche

If you haven't already done this on your own, take a moment now to answer these questions as honestly as you can. Doing so can clear your head about any doubts you may have about your future as a writer.

1. Are you hoping writing will help you get rich quick (or some variation thereof)?
a. No, money isn't my main goal.
b. Yes, my main motivation for writing is to make money.

2. Do you hope that writing will make you famous (or at least help you "be seen")?
a. I'd love to be a famous writer, but I still enjoy writing no matter what.
b. If I don't gain fans with my writing, I don't know if I'll want to continue.

3. How do you feel about spending hours alone with your laptop or pen/paper?
a. I'm okay with it.
b. I think I'll go stir-crazy.

4. Do you imagine that living the life of a writer comes complete with endless hours of daydreaming at some enticing location?
a. I like the idea, but I realize that's not reality for most writers.

b. I have those fantasies when I think of being a writer.

5. How do you feel about taking the time and effort that's necessary to improve as a writer?
a. I'm ready to put in the work, and I understand I'll need to practice and get feedback on my writing.
b. I just want to write what I write. I don't care what people think.

6. How would you draw the strength to proceed if you felt unappreciated?
a. As long as I know my work has value, I can proceed without too many pats on the back.
b. If I don't feel my work is appreciated, I can lose my motivation and would rather do something else.

7. How does the simple act of writing affect you?
a. There's something so very special about it that draws me.
b. It feels more like a chore than something I really want to do.

Now, tally up your answers:
_____ As _____ Bs

If you chose more As than Bs, the writing life will be rewarding for you. If you chose more Bs, take some time to think about being a writer. You don't want to spend your life doing something that doesn't bring you joy.

FOURTEEN

Your World Without Writing

WHETHER YOU HAVE ALREADY MADE your decision to pursue a life as a writer or are still unsure, it's worth pondering what your world would be like without writing. Warning: this may feel a little scary, particularly if you already identify as a writer and feel unsettled at the idea of giving it up. Don't worry, though. We're just playing pretend here, imagining what it might be like to leave writing behind. I encourage you to take an unbiased approach to this chapter, as it should help you feel confident and secure when making this important decision.

Seven Benefits of Leaving Writing Behind

1. You'll Have More Time for Other Things

For many writers, this is the most obvious benefit of stepping away from writing. Ah, the time! We devote countless hours to the craft, let alone building an author platform and marketing our work. The thought of having all that time for other activities is tempting.

You could work at making some of your other dreams come true, spend more time with family members, restart old projects you never completed, or even catch up on your sleep. You'd have time to relax on the weekends, go out with friends on weeknights, or enjoy binge-watching your favorite television show without feeling guilty. Sounds good, right?

Action Step: Consider what it would be like to reclaim the time you now devote to your writing career. Write down five things you would do if you had that time free. For example, "I'd have time to plant a garden," or "I'd have more time to play sports with my friends."

2. You'll Feel Less Pressure

We writers typically put a lot of pressure on ourselves to produce the best stories we can. This pressure doesn't let up when our work goes out into the world, either, as we take on even more pressure trying to get the word out and hoping readers will like it. Then there's the pressure to continue to build our author platforms so that new readers will discover our stories.

Imagine if all that pressure was lifted off your shoulders. No more worries about pleasing readers. No more trying to market your work. No more blogging, sending emails, and interacting on social media. You'd walk away feeling a new lightness in your being. No longer would it matter what readers think or how many comments or likes you'd get on your newsletter. You'd be free.

Action Step: Write down five ways this decision would benefit your well-being. Would you experience less daily stress and anxiety? Would it be easier to accept yourself without worrying about being judged by your readers? Would you enjoy escaping the constant pressure to be a good writer?

3. You Won't Have to Work So Hard

It takes hard work to succeed at pretty much anything, but to be a successful writer is even harder. On top of that, writing is often thankless work. Much like housework or yard work, you do it for little to no outside reward, perhaps for a significant length of time. Plus, you're never finished. It's not like you write a book, publish it, and live the good life forever after. There is always the next book to write, another blog to post, another workshop to attend, and another giveaway to organize. There is no official resting period and no ultimate destination.

Decide not to be a writer, and you may live an easier life—one that isn't defined by deadlines or worries about missing writing sessions, or guilt over not doing enough to promote your book.

Action Step: When you imagine a life less filled with writing work, what benefits do you think you would enjoy? Write down at least five ways you believe your mental, physical, or spiritual self would benefit if you could enjoy more leisure time instead of working so hard on your writing projects.

4. You'll Experience Fewer Emotional Ups and Downs

The writing life is an emotional one. Some days you feel great, and others you're down in the dumps. Such is life in general, but writers tend to have higher highs and lower lows. Here's why.

When you receive a good book review, you want to shout it from the rooftops. A bad one, though, may cause you to wonder why you ever thought you could be a writer. Some writing sessions leave you feeling elated, while others make you want to toss your laptop out the window. A simple word of praise can boost your spirits for weeks, while a single criticism can result in a month-long funk. Sometimes you'll believe in your work, and then you won't. You'll trust in your muse one moment, and then lose all sense of confidence the next. You can experience small triumphs over the course of many years only to suffer a serious setback that will have you second-guessing everything you've done.

According to writer, editor, and publisher Karen Gowen, "It takes an emotionally healthy person to withstand the intense demands: rigorous editing when their words are being challenged or perhaps cut entirely; after publication if sales don't meet expectations; and then having to follow up with another book if a sequel was planned. . . . The publishing process can bring even the best of us to our knees."

So be forewarned: the writing life is not for the faint of heart. At some point, it will knock you down, and it will be entirely up to you whether you can find the strength to get back up. The writing life can be a source of pure joy and a brutal weapon of destruction, a way to transcend the mortal coil and a heavy anchor dragging you down into the depths of despair. As a writer, you will experience the full range of emotions.

Are you ready for that?

Action Step: This isn't about emotional fortitude, though that will come into play if you decide to move forward. Rather, it's about the type of life you want to live. So ask yourself this: "Is it worth it to subject myself to the emotional ups and downs that come with being a writer? Will I get enough in return to strain my emotional well-being this way?"

5. You'll Find an Easier Way to Make Money

Every writer believes they are the exception to the rule and will beat the odds to rise to the top of an ever-expanding market and earn lots of money with their work. But as writer Susannah Breslin wrote in *Forbes* online, this isn't the way it goes for most of us.

"Odds are, you never will [earn millions of dollars]. This is your roulette wheel, and when it lands on every number but the one you picked, and you realize that after years of work, you haven't made more than a pittance at what you thought would be your new career, you will call it a day. Because you didn't have 'it.' . . . And you will see you should have picked something else: something easier, something less complicated, something other than a writer."

In real life, there are much easier ways to make money than writing books. Just look around. Pick something. Chances are it will be easier. Of course, that's not to say you can't make money as a writer. Of course you can; we've covered that in previous chapters. But it is far from easy.

Action Step: Imagine what life might be if you don't need to worry about making a living with your writing. What would you do instead? Would it fulfill you emotionally as well as financially? Write down at least three ways outside of writing in which you could make a living or make extra money on the side. Give each idea a rating from 1 to 10, with 1 meaning "not exciting" and 10 meaning "exciting." Then take some time to reflect on what your answers mean. If none of them were exciting, that's okay. Take note of that as well. But if any of them were exciting, consider whether they might be worth pursuing.

6. You Won't Have to Read So Much

If you decide to stay on the writing path, you'll be reading—a lot. Your work. Other authors' work. Blog posts. Social media posts. Books and articles about writing. Journals, e-newsletters, and more.

Successful writers are voracious readers for a reason. It's imperative to know all you can about your profession, and successful writers can tell you about every bestseller that dropped this year plus all the ones in their chosen genre from years past. They're also über-readers, meaning they devour books faster than Bart Simpson scarfs down burgers. They have an undying appetite for stories and the written word in general. If you took this away from them, they'd struggle to survive. Reading feeds the very essence of their being.

When you come down to it, it makes sense that writers love to read. Just as pilots love planes and farmers love animals, writers love books; and that love sustains them throughout their careers.

Action Step: Tally the number of books you read last year, last quarter, and last month. What do these totals tell you? Then imagine not feeling guilty about the books you didn't get around to reading. Does the thought lift a weight from your shoulders?

7. You Won't Have to Be Someone You're Not

There's no shame in giving something a try and then finding it's not for you. I experienced this when I took flying lessons. I loved every minute, even my solo flight. But I also discovered I wasn't really a pilot. I loved the freedom of flying, but not the technical aspects of it or the idea of having to face and manage a serious emergency. I treasure my experience to this day but I have no plans to pilot a plane regularly.

Writing can be looked at the same way. Maybe you've given it a try but are not so sure whether doing it regularly is right for you. That's okay. Tap into those feelings and respect them. Don't fight them, because they are trying to tell you something. Accept them and allow them to evolve. If, in the end, they lead you to decide you're not a writer, it means you'll now have the time to discover your true path—and that's a good thing.

Action Step: Block out everything else, and think only about the process of writing itself. When you're writing, do you feel like "you"? Does it bring you more in touch with your inner self? Does this feeling make you feel comfortable in a writer's skin? Or do you feel like you're fighting something inside you, like you're trying to be something you're not? Think of how it might affect you to let that feeling go.

Moving On with No Regrets

If, after exploring all the potential benefits, you've imagined putting writing behind you, it's time to make sure you'll have no regrets. Hopefully, you followed the prompts and answered the questions, so you have some of your thoughts down on paper and can review them.

This is important, as it's common for writers to toy with the idea of quitting at least once or twice during their careers. Maybe you've said something like, "I'm fed up with it, and I'm going to quit!" If so, in this section, we'll explore that scenario in-depth as a close-to-foolproof way to determine just how devoted to writing you are (or aren't).

No matter how you feel, let's assume that, at this point, the idea of giving up on writing and trying something else appeals to you. You've considered the benefits—and some of them look pretty attractive—and now you're curious to try it out. Before you do, take a few minutes to make sure you won't regret your decision. You can always go back to writing. But for now, if you're considering leaving it behind, it's helpful to ensure you're making the right decision for the right reasons.

There's been a lot of media coverage on regrets over the past few years, sparked mainly by Bronnie Ware's book, *The Top Five Regrets of the Dying: A Life Transformed by the Dearly Departing*. After years of working as a palliative nurse, tending to the needs of the dying, Bronnie found her life transformed and later wrote a popular blog post about the most common regrets she'd heard from her patients. That later evolved into her book. Curiously enough, many of these regrets are similar to those writers may have, as they focus on the same key areas: finding meaning, trusting ourselves, and having the courage to go after what we want.

Therefore, it's now time for your final test and a deeper dive into why writing matters in your life—or why it may not be your true calling.

1. Not Going After Your Dream

One of the most common regrets at the end of life is not going after your dreams. The reasons are many, from trying to be practical to not believing you can do it to wanting to live up to someone else's expectations of who you should be. In all cases, dreams are put on the back burner until it's too late.

Will you regret it? Do you dream of being a writer? Has this been your dream for some time? Will you feel bad if you let this dream go?

2. Not Having More Meaningful Work

Another common regret is not pursuing more meaningful work. People often stick with a dead-end job because it pays the bills, has retirement or healthcare benefits, or instills a sense of safety and security. The time is never right to pursue something more meaningful because it doesn't provide as well monetarily or doesn't afford the same lifestyle to which they've grown accustomed.

Will you regret it? Does writing bring meaning to your life? If so—

and if you let it go—are you confident about finding another type of meaningful work?

3. Worrying About What Others Think

Most of us worry about what others think of us on some level, particularly when we're starting out. I kept my writing to myself for years for a variety of reasons, most of them having something to do with others' opinions. This stemmed mostly from my worry that others wouldn't think I was any good at it, so I didn't want them reading my work. I was also concerned others would question *why* I was writing when there was no logical reason that I should. I wrongly assumed they would think it foolish and silly that I was spending so much time on such a fanciful dream.

When you sit down to write, do you hear someone else's voice in your head questioning or discouraging you? Be careful. Placing too much importance on what others think and not enough on what *you* think is one of the common regrets people have as they get older. Sure, in the moment, the opinions of others may seem important to your success and happiness. But at the end of life, what will matter most is whether you stayed true to yourself.

Will you regret it? Imagine you're ninety years old, with only days left to live. As you look back on your life and your decision not to pursue writing, discounting everyone else's opinions, do you think you will regret not pursuing your writing dreams?

4. Choosing the "Practical" Option

Though you may not be considering writing as a wage-earning occupation, you may still regret leaving it behind if your life is bound by practicalities.

When concerns about paying the bills, stocking the cupboards, and family safety take precedence, they tend to rule all your decisions. If you are the one who chooses to forego a beach vacation to save money for your child's braces, stay in a job you don't like to put your kids through college, or put off retirement to fix the roof instead of pursuing your dreams, you're being practical. But you may regret some of those decisions in the end.

Of course, making practical decisions is necessary; and much of the time, it cannot be avoided. Sometimes, however, it pays to take a risk. Cutting back on your hours (and your paycheck) for more time to devote to writing might not seem practical, but imagine how you'll feel within a year or so when you have a novel to show for it.

Will you regret it? Divide a sheet of paper into three columns. In the first one, write at least five decisions you've made concerning your writing. They don't have to be momentous decisions. Examples may include whether you wrote today, whether you made a change in your life to allow more time to write, or whether you took a risk and attended a writing conference even though your budget didn't allow for it. In the second column, write whether each decision was practical or impractical. In the third column, write what your ninety-year-old self would think of that decision. Finally, ask yourself, "What did this exercise point out about the price of *always* being practical?"

5. Spending Too Much Time Worrying

The older we get, the more we regret this one. Because after many years on this earth, we learn that what we worry about rarely occurs—and that all the time spent worrying is time wasted.

I'm a worrywart, and I'm well aware of how much needless anxiety and stress it causes. Some of my worries stem from choosing to be a freelance writer rather than a full-time employee. The freelance life is not secure and safe. Clients come and clients go, and there is no regular salary or benefits to fall back on. It's not lost on me that it's ironic that a worrywart would choose this sort of career, but I did it because I desperately wanted freedom and flexibility in my schedule—mainly, to accommodate my writing dreams. In truth, I've never once regretted this choice, because it has given me the time I wanted for my writing projects. I would have regretted far more taking a secure job that robbed me of time to write. Nevertheless, I still worry, and I'm working on doing less of that!

You, too, may struggle with worry; and you may come to regret the time you spent worrying when you get older. The important thing is to not let your worries rule your decisions when it comes to your writing.

Will you regret it? Write down the three main worries you have right now that are related to writing. Maybe you're worried that you won't be any good at it, or that it will take too much of your time away from your family. Acknowledge these worries, then challenge them by asking yourself, "Are they worth my time and energy? Will I one day come to regret that I gave them so much power over my decisions?"

6. Playing It Too Safe

Most humans prefer to play it safe most of the time. But on their deathbeds, they regret not taking more risks. This is an important regret for writers to consider, because in living the writing life, pretty much everything involves risk, including the following:

- Thinking you may have writing potential. What if you're wrong?
- Spending so much time writing. What if, in the end, the results disappoint you?
- Showing others your writing. What if they don't like it?
- Publishing your writing. What if you get bad reviews?
- Telling people you're a writer. What if they scoff and think you've just got a big ego?
- Submitting your writing to contests. What if your work is ignored?
- Spending your life writing. What if your only reward is the joy of the process?

Taking risks is scary for anyone and requires courage. Later in life, people look back and wish they'd been more courageous and taken more risks. From their vantage point, it's easier to see that it's better to take risks and fail than to never try. What we can also learn from the older generation is that the feeling of never having tried something can gnaw at a person like a wound that won't heal, whereas failure can be confronted and overcome. In the end, taking risks teaches us much more than playing it safe ever will.

Will you regret it? Think back on your experience as a writer. Recall at least three risks you've taken. They can be simple risks, like showing your work to a family member or friend or attending a writing workshop. How did taking each risk turn out? Looking back, are you glad you took the chance? Or do you wish you had chosen the safer route?

7. Not Trusting Your Inner Voice

We all have an inner voice that helps guide us toward our highest purpose in life, but many of us don't trust it or are afraid to listen to what it has to say. This may be because we don't believe we deserve to have the life we really want. But it's more likely that we discount what this inner voice is saying as being wrong and listen to the advice of others instead.

If you have a problem with the concept of an inner voice, imagine two voices inside your head. One voice favors stability; the other, authenticity. Our culture is big on being authentic, but think of how many choices you have made that favor stability instead. Being authentic means being true to yourself—and that often requires risk, which can quickly push you into instability.

It's not always comfortable to make the choices that support your heart's desire. Don't imagine that, because something is frightening or anxiety-producing, it's the wrong choice. Our intuition often pushes us to do the things that frighten us most, like trying to be a writer. If you want to live with fewer regrets, listen to the voice that favors authenticity.

Will you regret it? Think back on your life so far, and focus on the times when you *knew* instinctively what to do. Did you do it? Or did you let a desire for stability pull you in a different direction?

Now, focus on your writing life so far. Are you inclined to trust your inner voice? Remember—this is *your* life. Have the courage to take responsibility and make it truly your own.

Will You Regret It?

This chapter was designed to help you feel one of the following:

1. Sure that you want to be a writer and positive that you no longer want to think about quitting.
2. Sure that you don't want to be a writer—and grateful to realize this before devoting too much time to it.

Whichever decision fits you, it's time now to put that decision into your own words. It doesn't have to be profound, but it must be true and along these lines: "I've decided the writing life isn't for me," or "I'm finally going to write that novel I've been planning for years," or "I'm going to commit to building my author platform to attract more readers."

Now, put that decision in your own words. Write down your sentence, and place it in front of you.

Next, close your eyes and imagine yourself in a hospital bed. You're ninety years old and looking back on your life. Remember how you felt at this very moment when you made this decision about writing. Then, still using your imagination, answer the following questions:

- What was your life like as a result of this decision?
- What in your life changed because of this decision?
- Did you make the right decision?

FIFTEEN

Embrace the Life of a Writer

AS I THINK BACK on my decision to embrace the life of a writer, I don't see one particular moment accompanied by a metaphorical flash of lightning or a rumble of thunder. The decision came over me softly and quietly, like a quilt pulled up over my shoulders as I slept. Gradually, I came to realize that it was there, supporting me, fending off self-doubt, and encouraging me to keep going during difficult times. Gone was the indecision and questioning, leaving a peaceful commitment in its place. No longer did the whims of the marketplace cause me to distrust my priorities or my devotions. No more did the opinions of others matter more than my own. Instead, there was an abiding love of writing that now permeated everything, allowing me to focus all my energy on the one thing that mattered: becoming the best writer I could be.

Reaching this point in my writing life, as you've probably learned from this book, was anything but easy. I'm sure you've faced similar challenges along the way. I hope that, after reading the previous chapters and doing the exercises, you're feeling at least some of the quiet certainty I felt once I made this big decision. If you've decided that living life as a writer is for you no matter what, welcome to the select group of lifetime writers. You're one of those who have writing in their

DNA. You are dedicated to your craft even if you never earn a dime from it, and you believe that writing matters and has value far beyond the marketplace. I see you, and I'm so happy for you because I know the wonderful journey that lies ahead for you.

But I want you to be realistic about this decision because chances are there will be times even after this when you doubt whether you should continue writing or wonder when you can finally rest confidently in your identity as a writer. Even after you decide that writing is for you, the difficulties you'll face as a writer will still be there. But they will be less disruptive, allowing joy to take priority.

Embracing the Writing Life in Five Steps

The following five steps are designed to help you embrace a life of a writer by giving you a welcome sense of inner peace. So follow them, and shed any indecision and doubt as you confirm this important life choice.

1. Accept Yourself and Your Desire to Write

This one is hard because, in the beginning, we all wonder whether we have the talent to write or if we're wasting our time. This book should have given you a head start on this point, and hopefully, you've worked through that feeling of doubt. The most important thing you must do now is to fully embrace and accept your desire to write and allow it to permeate your being.

Accepting yourself as a writer doesn't mean you won't have days when you may question your choice, particularly when the money, notoriety, or other outside rewards that our culture bestows on its stars haven't yet come to you. Part of accepting yourself as a writer demands that your commitment be completely unaffected by outside forces. This is *your* life. You want to write, and it doesn't matter if you aren't famous. You are a writer, and no one else has anything to say about it. You want life as a writer, and that's enough. That's all that's required. Accept yourself and your desire to write, wholly and completely. Believe in yourself and your choice, and know that you made the right decision for yourself.

You should do something to mark this acceptance. Gift yourself an engraved pen or mug that says something like, "I am a writer," or "I choose to write." Then create a real writing nook in your home to acknowledge your commitment. Invest in a writing workshop or conference. The point is to do something to show you're no longer fighting this part of yourself, to show you're embracing it. Give your writer self a big hug and say, "Welcome home."

2. Focus on Growth Rather than Money or Fame

We all hope our writing will bring us outside rewards like money and fame. But while you're trying to grow your readership or find recognition through winning a contest, remember these activities—while perfectly worthwhile—are not as important as your growth as a writer.

When you get to a ripe old age and look back on your life, sure, those outside rewards will bring back good memories. But imagine the pride and joy that can come from having mentored other writers or completed the story you longed to write. Imagine yourself not just as the writer you are right now, but as your future self who has become the master you can only dream about today.

Focusing on growth as your major goal helps you in these ways:

- It keeps disappointments related to money and fame from growing out of proportion.
- It sustains your joy in writing.

When you focus on honing your craft, you can enjoy the thrill when you portray a character just right, your plot falls into place, your description makes your fictional setting seem real, or your dialogue sounds authentic. Focusing on learning transports your thoughts to a healthier place, making you a happier writer who is less buffeted about by reviews and/or sales.

Continue to invest in your education. Don't hesitate to take classes, read another writing book, attend another conference, or hire an editor. Never stop learning. It's the journey, not the destination, that makes the artist. When your joy comes from doing the work to gradually master your craft, it's the deepest joy there is. The more you work to reach that point, the sweeter your rewards will be.

3. Build Your Platform Your Way

One of the main reasons writers get discouraged is because they run up against a wall trying to market their books. This is completely understandable, and it's also something you can fix when you have the desire to keep writing.

Writers as a whole know nothing about marketing, as it's a learned skill. It's not something you can magically do on your own. You need someone to teach you how to do it. Plus, you need to practice various methods to find those that work best for you. What's harder to process is that the success (read: sales) of your book depends on how well it's marketed. Yet most writers don't even start learning about marketing until after they publish a book. That's like trying to learn karate while in the ring, fighting an opponent. Unfortunately, most of us writers end up excited and proud of publishing a book, then stressed and overwhelmed at the prospect of trying to market it.

To avoid becoming that exhausted, discouraged writer with a book that's languishing on the shelves, it helps to start marketing yourself earlier. But let's be frank: new writers are more focused on learning how to *write*. If you're fortunate and can begin your marketing education before you publish, terrific. This gives you an advantage, but one that comes with its own pitfalls. It's putting the cart before the horse to think too much about sales before mastering the art of storytelling. One could argue that such a split mindset robs a writer of the patience and focus needed to become the best writer possible.

The cold, hard reality is that this is publishing in today's world. If you're in a position where you can afford to hire a marketing consultant or pay for marketing services, by all means, do it. If not, start taking classes and talking to other writers, but realize that learning to market your books will take time. Fortunately, you have a lifetime to spend writing, so try to relax and go step by step. Read books. Take courses. Blog to build an audience. Write articles for online magazines and journals. Try a variety of techniques—anything to build a platform—and see what works for you.

This leads us to the point of this step: you must discover the type of marketing that *you* enjoy and that suits your work. There are standard marketing techniques that are often touted as helping authors increase sales. These may include running Amazon and Facebook ads, conducting giveaways, setting up book blog tours, getting onto book promo sites, blogging, sending out e-newsletters, and more. It doesn't do you or your work any good, however, to try to stuff yourself into a mold that doesn't fit. If you don't *enjoy* a particular marketing technique, it will show—and you won't get very good results. That, in turn, can give you the impression that no one likes your book when the real problem is that your marketing isn't working and few people know about you or your work.

Marketing shouldn't feel like drudgery or make you into something you're not. You can absolutely share news about your work in ways that don't strike you as slimy or salesy, so don't get caught up in that common roadblock. In embracing the life of a writer, you must also embrace the fact that you'll need to market your work. The key is to market *your way* so that these marketing activities are rewarding for you.

4. Embrace the Difficulty

I've never met a writer who said that the writing life is easy. Often, all writers can talk about is how difficult it is. First, there's the writing itself. Then there is the editing. If you make it through the initial draft (woo-hoo!), it's time to go back and pound it into shape. This often turns into writing multiple drafts. Then it's time to let other people—beta readers, editors, mentors—read it. Getting their feedback is often as much fun as getting a root canal. Once you let their criticisms sink in, it's time to peel your ego off the floor and write the next (and hopefully final) draft.

When that draft is finished, you can go out and celebrate. But don't get too comfortable, because now starts the publication process. Whether you seek a traditional publisher or publish it yourself, you must go through several more steps before you can hold a finished book. If publishing traditionally, you must research publishers, submit and submit, wait, and submit again—and hopefully one day, you'll be offered a contract. Now it's time to dive into more revising to accommodate additional edits, notes, and queries from the copy editor and perhaps questions from the proofreader, all while doing everything you can to build some buzz for the book.

Self-publishing means you must wear all the hats as you dive into editing and production mode, either by outsourcing or taking on every task: designing the cover, completing the final edits and proofreading, designing the interior, obtaining your ISBNs, writing the back cover copy, finding your keywords, creating new website pages, and finally uploading the final book files to your distributor(s).

Along the way, you will face setbacks. You could get stuck in the middle of your story and not know how to finish it, struggle to make crucial edits, or get discouraged and feel like the story will never work. Then there's real life. You might experience trauma and have to set your work aside for a while, only to return to it and find that you forgot where you were going.

When you finally publish, there are more challenges. Marketing tasks must be shoehorned into your busy schedule, which can leave the most hardened souls feeling overwhelmed and stressed out. The book launch might not go as well as planned, or the book might not receive uniformly glowing reviews. Or it might not sell as well as expected, and that means a short self-life, as they say in the business (unless you self-published, which means more and better marketing is needed).

When it's all over, you'll be faced with the task of doing it all over again!

The writing life is not for wimps. But when you feel compelled to write, trust me, you will come to embrace the difficulty. We writers wear our scars with pride, from the ones we get from each rejection or one-star review to the ones inflicted by unsuitable writing mentors to those we inflict on ourselves (like when we give up on a novel).

Struggles and difficulties build character. It's true! You'll find that most lifetime writers are extremely supportive and encouraging of other writers. We band together for strength because we all know how tough it is. As in life, there are no guarantees of outward success, but there is valor in giving it a go. So embrace the struggle. Let it shape and mold you. If you don't give up, one day you'll admire the writer you have become.

5. Cultivate the Joy

Nothing can compare to getting so immersed in a story that you lose track of time. Nothing else can give you that feeling of elation that washes over you when typing the words *The End*. I challenge you to tell me what else can help heal your aching soul like a story pouring from your heart, or what else thrills you as much as taking a ride on a dragon with your heroine or zipping through the city streets on the back of your hero's motorcycle.

That's the power of writing. If you're to thrive on the long and often difficult journey that is the writing life, you must continually nurture that joy. When things go wrong, return to the work. When the bad review comes in, or when no one seems to care about your blog, return to the work. Your writing is where you'll cultivate the joy that will sustain and entertain you.

I have my writing to thank for so many of the meaningful experiences in my life. There I found healing, self-confidence (even as it coexists with self-doubt), transcendence, validation, and understanding. My writing life has connected me with amazing people from whom I've learned so much. It's taken me to places I never would have gone otherwise and helped me discover new strengths I didn't know I had.

To succeed as a lifelong writer, it's paramount to pay significant attention to the many benefits writing is capable of delivering. Find joy in small successes and celebrate your achievements. Take the time to nurture this part of yourself even more than you think you should. Take yourself out on writing dates where you focus on nothing but following your imagination. Go on writing retreats. Attend writing conferences. Travel to do research. Set up a writing nook that's comfortable and conducive to creativity. Follow a routine that helps you stay healthy and motivated to write. Meet regularly with other writers so you can encourage each other. Read the books and see the movies that will inspire you.

Take action to care for your inner writer. It's not selfish or indulgent—on the contrary. If you expect to continue producing while starving yourself of creative nourishment, all you'll succeed in doing is driving yourself smack into a wall. To keep joy front and center in your writing life, take those actions that will nourish the writer inside. Never lose sight of the fact that you chose writing because you could see how it benefits you. Make it a priority to recognize those benefits when they come along. Take time to celebrate them and bask in the joy they give you.

∽

Are You Ready to Embrace the Life of a Writer?

We're nearing the end of our journey, which means it's time to ask yourself the big question: Are you ready to embrace the life of a writer? Choose your answer:

_____ Yes _____ No

Next, it's time to rate the emotion you just felt when you answered that question with a number between 1 and 5, with 1 meaning "little to no emotion" and 5 meaning "lots of emotion." If you're ecstatic about embracing the life of a writer, for example, your rating would be a 5. Feeling positive but not super positive might rate as a 3 or a 4. The same applies if your answer was no. A determined "Heck no!" would rate as a 5. An "I don't think so" may rate as a 2 or 3.

Circle your rating: 1 2 3 4 5

The stronger the emotion, the more decisive your answer. Yes or no, you've made a decision and are now ready to move on. But if you're stuck in the middle range, your emotions are less powerful and you still have more thinking to do. That's okay. Nothing is saying you *have* to decide by the end of this book.

Instead, use this rating to help you gain a better idea of where you are at this point. If it is squarely in the "I'm still not 100 percent positive" realm, you can keep mulling over the things we've talked about until the answer becomes clear one day. Be patient and follow your heart.

Yes or no, either way, you've made a decision. Go confidently in that direction and see what happens. If you're not pleased with the outcome, you can always adjust your course.

SIXTEEN

The Reason Why You Write

THERE IS A WELL-KNOWN quote that's often attributed to John Pierpont Morgan: "A man always has two reasons for doing anything: a good reason, and the real reason." Morgan was a banker, but this quote holds true for any action—even writing, as you may well know. We all have our good reasons for writing, the ones we tell others when they ask why we write. Common examples include "I've always enjoyed telling stories," "I like the challenge," and "It's a great creative outlet." Others reasons range from earning money on the side to preserving family memories to addressing issues we're passionate about.

These are all good reasons to write. And who's to say which ones are good versus which ones are real? Well, only you. As the quote implies, your good reasons may not be the real reasons you feel called to write—or why your writing matters enough to you to keep doing it. You may insist that your good reasons are true because you like telling stories. I believe you, but I'm also willing to bet there's something deeper that's driving you, something you may not even be aware of. If you've decided that writing *is* for you, then try to answer the question, "Why?" Delving deep into your motivation to write will help you to understand your real reason, allowing you to feel more grounded in your identity as a writer.

Don't be surprised if this doesn't happen overnight, particularly when it comes to your real reason. It can be elusive and is often buried so deep in the unconscious mind that unearthing it takes time, experience, and (often) suffering. When your story is rejected by the twentieth agent and you muster the courage to turn around and send it out again, you may unearth the real reason. When you launch a book to poor reviews and find the strength to go back and start working on your next book, you may notice the real reason motivating you. When you struggle with a story for years yet have the resilience to keep trying, that's your real reason at work.

People often have hidden reasons for doing things. Consider the person who is always late. When asked why, "good reasons" include running late at work, dealing with traffic jams, and losing track of time. Psychologists say, however, that often the real reason is that some people simply hate being early. They may not enjoy waiting because it is an inefficient use of time. They may feel awkward and uneasy while waiting and doing nothing. They don't want to be the "nerd" who comes early.

Hidden reasons are also likely to drive the always-on-time counterparts. They claim to arrive promptly to respect other people's time. But in truth, they may worry that arriving a minute or two late will cause others to think less of them. Perhaps they have bad memories of being late for school or feel that being on time means never missing out on anything.

The point is that humans are commonly driven to do things for reasons we don't understand. One frequently dispensed piece of advice is to "do what makes you happy." If you applied that advice to writing, however, you might find yourself confused. No doubt writing makes you happy sometimes, but it's also likely to generate a myriad of other emotions from sad to elated to depressed. Does that mean writing isn't valuable, because it doesn't always make us happy? Indeed, that's one of the reasons it *is* so valuable, which is a prime example of why we should be careful about blindly following this type of advice.

But if writing is not always a source of happiness, that brings us back to the question of why it's worthwhile doing. Of course, if you answer along the lines of "Because nothing else fulfills me as writing does," or "Because when I'm writing, everything else falls away," or "Nothing feels as honest and true as writing does," then you have a clue.

As for my own real reason for writing, I'm still digging. But I sense it has something to do with feeling most myself when sharing with the blank page. I still refer to Andre Dubus III's quote from his memoir, *Townie*, as I can't say it any better: "And I felt more like me than I ever had, as if the years I'd lived so far had formed layers of skin and muscle over myself that others saw as me when the real one had been underneath all along. . . ."

Your real reason is unique to you alone, even if it's not quite evident right now. If you've come to the end of this book and decided your writing does matter, I hope that you'll honor that decision. Trust that it comes from the deepest part of your being, a part that may still be evolving and will continue to do so over the coming years. Enjoy the metamorphosis.

No matter what happens, no matter the outside rewards (or lack thereof), when you make writing a priority in your life, your life will be better because of it.

Hang in there. You'll see.

Appendices

Note from the Author

Thank you for reading *Your Writing Matters!*

Reviews are gold to authors. If you've enjoyed this book, please consider rating and reviewing it on Amazon.com and/or Goodreads.com.

To learn more about empowering your wellness and creativity, sign up for the free *Writing and Wellness* newsletter at writingandwellness.com/newsletter. You'll gain access to inspirational and motivational posts, additional training, future books, and more.

Recommended Reading

Do less important tasks frequently flood your schedule and sink your creative motivation? Are you frustrated and out of touch with your inner artist? Do you wish you could create a calmer, more creative life so you could write without guilt?

Your rescue is here! After twenty years' experience in the writing industry, author Colleen M. Story extends a lifeline to pull you out of the sinking swamp of "busyness" and back into the flourishing creative life you deserve.

Overwhelmed Writer Rescue provides practical, personalized solutions to help beginning and experienced writers and other creative artists escape the tyranny of the to-do list to nurture the genius within. You'll find ways to boost productivity, improve time management, and restore your sanity while gaining insight into your unique creative nature and what it needs to thrive.

Ultimately, you'll discover what may be holding you back from experiencing the true joy that a creative life can bring.

Available now on Amazon and wherever books are sold!

Have you been writing for years, but feel like no one notices? Have you published your stories, only to gain a handful of readers? Do your marketing efforts feel like shouting into a void?

Veteran writer and motivational coach Colleen M. Story helps you break the spell of invisibility to reveal the author platform that will finally draw readers your way.

Writer Get Noticed! dispells the notion that fixing your writing flaws and expanding your social media reach will get you the readers you deserve. Instead, discover a myriad of strengths you didn't know you had, then use them to find your author theme, power up your platform, and create a new author business blueprint, all while gaining insight into what sets you apart as a writer and creative artist.

Writers need readers to achieve their highest potential. Find your way to stand out, and let it lead you to the writing career that fulfills all your expectations and more.

Available now on Amazon and wherever books are sold!

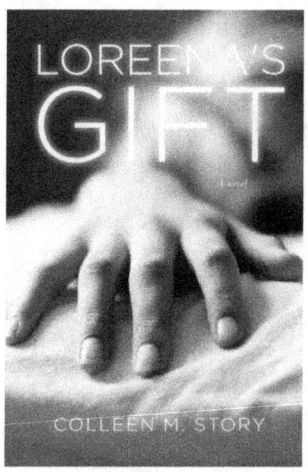

A blind girl's terrifying "gift" allows her to regain her eyesight—but only as she ferries the recently deceased into the afterlife.

Loreena Picket thinks she knows herself. A blind young woman who lives with her uncle, a reverend at a small-town church, she's a dutiful niece and talented pianist for the congregation.

But they're both hiding a terrible secret. Loreena can kill people with the touch of her hand.

While her uncle sees her as an angel of mercy, helping usher the terminally ill members of his flock into the afterlife, Loreena has her doubts.

Torn between doing her uncle's bidding and the allure of the fleeting moments when her eyesight returns on the journey to the other side, Loreena cooperates with her uncle until her troubled older brother returns to town. When she reveals her power by saving him from a local drug dealer, she is drawn into a sinister and dangerous world that will test the true nature of her talent and force her to consider how far she is willing to go to survive.

An exciting debut that crosses fantasy and literary fiction, *Loreena's Gift* is a thought-provoking meditation on life and death and what ultimately lies beyond this world. Available now on Amazon or wherever books are sold.

Coming in Spring 2022:

The Beached Ones

He's determined to rescue his brother. But it isn't his brother who needs rescuing.

They grew up in an abusive home. Daniel escaped. Once established as a stunt rider, he intended to go back. But then one jump went horribly wrong….

In an unexplained twist of nature, he emerges unscathed, so he sets out to get his brother as planned. But soon, his reality begins to fall apart. His team mourns his passing. His best friend won't answer his calls. Strangers die in front of him. Even his girlfriend, the one person he thought he could trust, is hiding something.

Fighting his way through a fog of lost memories, he finally arrives at his destination: the Golden Gate Bridge. A place of beauty and despair, it shows him the truth he's been trying to avoid, and he must choose to let justice run its course or trust the bonds of brotherhood and take a leap of faith.

Coming soon from CamCat Books.

Featured Authors

Listed in order of appearance are the authors from Writing and Wellness who contributed their stories to this book. I offer my gratitude to each one of you!

Novelist, journalist, and ghostwriter **Holly Robinson** is the author of *The Gerbil Farmer's Daughter: A Memoir* and six novels. Her articles and essays appear regularly in national publications, and she is currently working on a new novel. Holly and her husband have five children and divide their time between Massachusetts and Prince Edward Island. www.authorhollyrobinson.com

Mona Ingram loves to make up stories and is the author of more than four dozen romances. Most mornings, she can be found at her computer, trying to keep up with the characters in her current work, many of whom invariably want to go off in a completely different direction than she planned. But that's the joy of writing. An avid bird watcher, Mona is particularly happy when she can combine bird watching with travel. www.monaingram.com

Natalie Cline Bright is an author, blogger, and speaker. She holds a BBA in business/marketing, enjoys talking to people of all ages about writing, and is the author of articles and books for kids and adults. Her new series, the Wild Cow Ranch, is a contemporary western Christian romance set on a cattle ranch in Texas. She blogs on her website every week about the people, places, and fascinating history of the Texas Panhandle. Find out more and sign up for her e-newsletter at www.nataliebright.com.

Lori Robinett has written several books, including *Fatal Impulse, Fatal Obsession, Diamond Hard, Denim & Diamonds, Diamond in the Rough,* and *Finding Clarity*. She also runs an online school, WriteScout, where she teaches writing one skill at a time. Her signature course is Blank to 50K: Draft Your Novel. Before she started writing for publication, Lori earned a bachelor's degree in education from the University of Central Missouri. After working in higher education for several years, she changed lanes and began working in the legal field. She's now living in the perfect world, working in the legal field for higher education. Lori lives in rural Missouri with her husband of over twenty-five years. If Lori isn't writing, you may find her reading or crafting. www.lorilrobinett.com

Jo Ann Simon, a corporate executive, is a lifelong Nutmegger, living in various locations in the Nutmeg State of Connecticut. She is a constant traveler, exploring the world including her favorite country, Italy. When she is not traveling, Jo Ann loves spending time with her family, friends, and her nine grandchildren. Her day job (where she runs a company), painting fine art, gardening, and writing fill in the blanks of her life. Palm trees are essential in her personal landscape, with beaches to match. www.joann-simon.com

Beth Castrodale worked as a newspaper reporter until her love of books led her to the publishing field. She was a senior editor at Bedford/St. Martin's and is the founding editor of Small Press Picks. Her short fiction and essays have appeared in numerous publications, including *Marathon Literary Review, Printer's Devil Review,* and *Smoky Blue Literary and Arts Magazine.* Her debut novel, *Marion Hatley,* was a finalist for a Nilsen Prize for a First Novel from Southeast Missouri State University Press. An excerpt from her second novel, *In This Ground,* was a shortlist finalist for a William Faulkner–William Wisdom Creative Writing Award. Her latest novel, *I Mean You No Harm,* is forthcoming from Imbrifex Books. www.bethcastrodale.com

Rebecca Whitehead Munn is passionate about rethinking what's possible and brings intellectual humility to all her endeavors. Her passion in writing is to demystify topics that we all face (such as death and cancer) and yet are challenged to talk about. She is an award-winning author of two books, *All of Us Warriors: Cancer Stories of Survival and Loss* (2020) and *The Gift of Goodbye: A Story of Agape Love* (2017). She has been a featured Maria Shriver Architect of Change on surviving grief and shared her healing through yoga story at www.-mindbodygreen.com. She is a certified end-of-life doula, certified in Positive Psychology, and a Nashville Healthcare Council Fellow. She is happiest spending time outdoors, being a mom, eating Mexican food, practicing yoga, listening to live music, and using her chaotic Aries energy for good. She has lived in Nashville, Tennessee, since 2005. www.rebeccawmunnauthor.com

Jane Nannono is a Ugandan medical doctor who has lived and worked in Uganda and Botswana. Her first fiction novel, *The Last Lifeline,* was published in 2015; and she self-published her second novel, *And The Lights Came On,* in 2016. Two of her short stories appeared in the Africa Book Club Anthology: Volume 1 (2014) entitled, *The Bundle of Joy and Other Stories from Africa.* Other stories of Jane's appear in the February 2020 edition of *Yours 2 Read,* a London-based online platform, and in the June 2020 issue of *Kalahari Review.* She is a member of the Africa Book Club, FEMRITE – Uganda Women Writers' Association, The Write Practice, and Two Drops of Ink. She is a strong supporter of women's empowerment and brings it out in the strong, independent female characters she creates. She writes African stories lived by

African characters mainly in Africa. She is a mother of two adorable sons and one daughter, a grandmother, and a guardian of two of her nieces. www.apagefrommunakusbook834350529.blog

Patty Somlo's most recent book, *Hairway to Heaven Stories*, was published by Cherry Castle Publishing, a Black-owned press committed to literary activism. *Hairway* was a finalist in the American Fiction Awards and Best Book Awards. Two of Somlo's previous books, *The First to Disappear* (Spuyten Duyvil) and *Even When Trapped Behind Clouds: A Memoir of Quiet Grace* (WiDo Publishing), were finalists in several book contests. Her work has appeared in *Guernica, Gravel, Sheepshead Review, Under the Sun, The Los Angeles Review,* and *The Nassau Review,* among others, and in over thirty anthologies. She received an honorable mention for fiction in the Women's National Book Association Writing Contest, was a finalist in the Parks & Points Essay Contest, had an essay selected as Notable for Best American Essays, and has been nominated for the Pushcart Prize multiple times as well as Best of the Net. www.pattysomlo.com

Founder of Watch God Work Ministries, **Rebecca Olmstead** is an award-winning author and prophetic intercessor. In her latest book, *Loved So Much It Hurts: Purpose in the Pain*, Rebecca shares her journey through cancer, her miraculous healing, and the spiritual transformation she experienced through it all. She has also released her award-winning story, "The Uninvited Guest: A Short Story," on Amazon. Her writing has appeared in The Upper Room, Focus on the Family's *Clubhouse Jr., Live, Now What?, Houseboat Magazine,* and on her online ministry, watchgodwork.com. She is currently working on a one-year devotional, *Promise of the Day: Power-Filled Devotions for Victorious Living*; a mystery series; and a collection of short stories. Rebecca loves teaching and inspiring others to go higher in the Spirit and deeper in the Word. She lives with her husband and the youngest of their five children in southeastern Washington. www.rebeccaolmstead.com

Ilene Birkwood has been lucky enough to live in some of the most beautiful and interesting places in the world: charming English villages, New Zealand's subtropical north, a beach paradise in Bermuda, and the excitement of Silicon Valley. These places make great locations for her books. She grew up on the Isle of Wight in England and later moved to California and joined Hewlett Packard. She became one of the first female managers at Hewlett Packard and, after a long career there, ended up as Vice President of Tandem Computers. In their mid-fifties, she and her husband returned to New Zealand, where she started writing. Now, she lives in the beautiful Pacific Northwest, a perfect spot for writing. She published her mysteries *Deadly Deception* in 2004, *What to Do About Emma* in 2015, and *Hidden Depths* in 2016. Her nonfiction book, *The Second Torpedo*, was published in 2012. *The Druids*, a description of the Druidic way of life, was published in 2020. www.ilenebirkwood.com

Sara Secora, the author of The Amethysta Trilogy, is a proclaimed wordsmith with a wildfire imagination. Her concocted ventures range widely, from being the poet behind *Dear Wallflower* to reaching an esteemed position as a professional voiceover actress. And if she didn't already wear enough creative hats, Sara can also be found working as a casting director and copywriter. Based in the heart of Detroit, Michigan, Sara is actively writing whimsical stories brimming with enchantment, mystique, and insight that are destined to intrigue readers of any age. www.sarasecora.com

Kai Raine is a writer and cognitive scientist who believes in the power of stories to help readers and writers alike to think outside the box and see past assumptions. Kai reads and writes to experience lives and opinions and possibilities beyond her own. She has lived a relatively nomadic life, being born in the United States, then growing up mostly in Japan and spending most of her early adult life in Europe. She has a Bachelor of Arts degree from the University of Alaska Fairbanks and Master of Science degrees from the University of Trento (Italy) and

Osnabrück University (Germany). Kai is the author of the fantasy novel *These Lies That Live Between Us*. www.kairaine.com

Crissi Langwell writes novels with genres that include romance, magical realism, women's fiction, and young adult. Her passion is the story of the underdog; and her novels tell stories of homeless teens, determined heroines, family issues, free spirits, and more. Beyond writing, Crissi is an avid bookworm and a yoga enthusiast. She pulls her inspiration from the ocean and breathes freely among redwoods. She lives in northern California with her husband and their blended family of three young adult kids and a spoiled, sassy cat. www.crissi-langwell.com

Elaine Mansfield's book *Leaning into Love: A Spiritual Journey through Grief* (Larson Publications) won the 2015 Gold Medal IPPY (Independent Publisher Book Award) for Aging, Death, and Dying. Her TEDx talk, "Good Grief! What I Learned from Loss," has over 260,000 views. Her essay "Wild Nights: Grief Dreams, Mythology, and the Inner Marriage" won first place in the 2016-17 C.G. Jung in the Heartland Writing Competition. Elaine follows her heart in writing. Along with a focus on grief, she's a student of nature, Jungian psychology, and meditation. She writes about renewal, dreams, mythology, and the environment; and she volunteers for hospice. Elaine raises monarch butterflies every summer and is focused on a personal guide with photos for protecting and releasing monarchs for migration in the northeastern United States. www.elainemansfield.com

Linda K. Sienkiewicz's poetry, short stories, essays, and art have been published in numerous literary journals and anthologies. Among her awards are a Hoffer Finalist award for her debut novel, *In the Context of Love*; a Pushcart Prize nomination; and a poetry chapbook award. She has three other poetry chapbooks. Her newest release is a children's picture book, *Gordy and the Ghost Crab*, which she wrote and illustrated. Her MFA is from Stonecoast at the University of Southern Maine. www.lindaksienkiewicz.com

Mary Avery Kabrich grew up in rural Minnesota and moved to Seattle when she was twenty-three, fulfilling her childhood desire of becoming an urban dweller. She spent all of elementary school confused about how everyone else had figured out the mysterious process of reading. *Once Upon a Time a Sparrow* is fiction informed by her life experiences as a child with severe dyslexia in the late '60s and early '70s, at a time and place when an inability to read was not understood. Mary has worked as a special education teacher, private tutor, and university instructor. She currently fulfills her passions serving students in the Seattle school district as a school psychologist and writing stories of transformation. www.maryaverykabrich.com

Karen Gowen loves to read and believes in the power of books to change lives, for they have changed hers. After raising her very large family, she finds it a joy and privilege to be writing full-time. She first began writing for publication when her children were young, selling children's stories to *The Friend* magazine. She just finished her seventh book, a self-help memoir called *Slim Within: 4 Rules of Eating 4 Permanent Weight Loss*. She's currently working on a memoir about her Guatemala experience. www.karenjonesgowen.com

References

Intro

Blumberg, Yoni. "College Students Today Value Education Less and Money More: Study." *CNBC*, November 3, 2017. https://www.cnbc.com/2017/11/03/college-students-today-value-education-less-and-money-more-study.html.

Cook, Eli. "How Money Became the Measure of Everything." *The Atlantic*, October 19, 2017. https://www.theatlantic.com/business/archive/2017/10/money-measure-everything-pricing-progress/543345/.

Ingraham, Christopher. "Americans Are Becoming Less Happy, and There's Research to Prove It." *Los Angeles Times,* March 23, 2019. https://www.latimes.com/science/sciencenow/la-sci-sn-americans-less-happy-20190323-story.html.

Monnot, Matthew J. "Marginal Utility and Economic Development: Intrinsic Versus Extrinsic Aspirations and Subjective Well-Being Among Chinese Employees." *Social Indicators Research* 132, no. 1 (2017): 155-185. https://doi:10.1007/s11205-015-1153-9.

Park, Lora E., Deborah E. Ward, and Kristin Naragon-Gainey. "It's All About the Money (For Some): Consequences of Financially Contingent Self-Worth." *Personality and Social Psychology Bulletin* 43, no. 5 (May 2017): 601-622. https://doi:10.1177/0146167216689080.

Schiller, Ben. "America, Desperate for Happiness, Is Getting Less and Less Happy." *Fast Company* (blog), March 16, 2018. https://www.fastcompany.com/40544341/america-desperate-for-happiness-is-getting-less-and-less-happy.

Twenge, Jean M., and Kristin Donnelly. "Generational Differences in American Students' Reasons for Going to College, 1971–2014: The Rise of Extrinsic Motives." *The Journal of Social Psychology*, 156, no. 6 (2016): 620-629. https://doi.org/10.1080/00224545.2016.1152214.

Chapter 1

Rahhal, Natalie. "How to Avoid Becoming Paralyzed by Indecision: Brain Scans and Vision Trackers Reveal How 'Learn' What to Like When We Make Hard Choices." *DailyMail.com*, December 11, 2018. https://www.dailymail.co.uk/health/article-6484523/Brain-scans-reveal-overcome-indecision-learn-like-good-choices.html.

Voigt, Katharina, Carsten Murawski, Sebastian Speer, and Stefan Bode. "Hard Decisions Shape the Neural Coding of Preferences." *The Journal of Neuroscience* 39, no. 4 (2018): 718-726. https://doi.org/10.1523/JNEUROSCI.1681-18.2018.

Winfrey, Oprah. *What I Know for Sure*. London: Pan Macmillan, 2014.

Chapter 2

BrainyQuote. "Talent is cheaper than table salt. What separates the talented individual from the successful one is a lot of hard work." Stephen King Quotes. Accessed October 28, 2020. https://www.brainyquote.com/quotes/stephen_king_163656.

Deen, Shulem. "Can Writing Be Taught—Or Must It Always Come Naturally?" *School of Nonfiction* (blog), *Shulem Deen*, March 21, 2018. https://shulemdeen.com/writing-taught/.

Duckworth, Angela. "FAQ: I Don't Understand What You Mean by 'Talent'?" AngelaDuckworth.com. Accessed April 3, 2020. https://angeladuckworth.com/qa/#faq-62.

Farland, David. "Can Writing Be Taught?" *My Story Doctor* (blog), April 11, 2019. https://mystorydoctor.com/can-writing-be-taught/.

Pressfield, Steven. "Nobody Knows Nothing." *Steven Pressfield* (blog), last modified January 29, 2014. https://stevenpressfield.com/2014/01/nobody-knows-nothing/.

Quast, Lisa. "Why Grit Is More Important Than IQ When You're Trying to Become Successful." *Forbes*, March 6, 2017. https://www.forbes.com/sites/lisaquast/2017/03/06/why-grit-is-more-important-than-iq-when-youre-trying-to-become-successful/#e5dab697e45c.

Chapter 3

The Authors Guild. "Authors Guild Survey Shows Drastic 42 Percent Decline in Authors Earnings in Last Decade." Last modified January 10, 2019. https://www.authorsguild.org/industry-advocacy/authors-guild-survey-shows-drastic-42-percent-decline-in-authors-earnings-in-last-decade/.

Bowker. "New Record: More Than 1 Million Books Self-Published in 2017." Last modified October 10, 2018. https://www.bowker.com/news/2018/New-Record-More-than-1-Million-Books-Self-Published-in-2017.html.

Dowden, Craig. "Why You Need to Be Seen." *Psychology Today* (blog), September 11, 2014. https://www.psychologytoday.com/us/blog/the-leaders-code/201409/why-you-need-be-seen.

Flood, Alison. "Most Writers Earn Less Than £600 a Year, Survey Reveals." *The Guardian*, January 14, 2014. https://www.theguardian.com/books/2014/jan/17/writers-earn-less-than-600-a-year.

Forgeard, Marie J., and Anne C. Mecklenburg. "The Two Dimensions of Motivation and a Reciprocal Model of the Creative Process." *Review of General Psychology* 17, no. 3 (2013): 255-266. https://doi.org/10.1037/a0032104.

Gander, Kashmira. "Americans Value Money More Than Friendship, Survey Reveals." *Newsweek*, November 23, 2018. https://www.newsweek.com/americans-value-money-more-friendship-survey-reveals-1228665.

Henderson, J. Maureen. "One in Four Millennials Would Quit Their Job to Be Famous." *Forbes*, January 24, 2017. https://www.forbes.com/sites/jmaureenhenderson/2017/01/24/one-in-four-millennials-would-quit-their-job-to-be-famous/#67ba0e952c43.

Hess, Abigail Johnson. "24 Percent of American Adults Haven't Read a Book in the Past Year—Here's Why." *CNBC*, January 29, 2019. https://www.cnbc.com/2019/01/29/24-percent-of-american-adults-havent-read-a-book-in-the-past-year--heres-why-.html.

Kaufman, Scott Barry. "Why Do You Want to Be Famous?" *Beautiful Minds* (blog), *Scientific American*, September 4, 2013. https://blogs.scientificamerican.com/beautiful-minds/why-do-you-want-to-be-famous/.

Kershaw, Allison. "Fame the Career Choice for Half of 16-Year-Olds." *The Independent*, February 17, 2010. https://www.independent.co.uk/news/education/education-news/fame-the-career-choice-for-half-of-16-year-olds-1902338.html.

Landau, Elizabeth. "How the 'Fame Motive' Makes You Want to Be a Star." *CNN*, October 28, 2009. https://www.cnn.com/2009/HEALTH/10/28/psychology.fame.celebrity/.

Leskin, Paige. "American Kids Want to Be Famous on YouTube, and Kids in China Want to Go to Space: Survey." *Business Insider*, July 17, 2019. https://www.businessinsider.com/american-kids-youtube-star-astronauts-survey-2019-7.

Lucas, Suzanne. "Americans Value Money over Time Off." *MoneyWatch* (blog), *CBS News*, February 28, 2014. https://www.cbsnews.com/news/americans-value-money-over-time-off/.

Michel, Lincoln. "Everything You Wanted to Know About Book Sales (But Were Afraid to Ask)." *Electric Literature*, June 30, 2016. https://electricliterature.com/everything-you-wanted-to-know-about-book-sales-but-were-afraid-to-ask/.

Neary, Lynn. "When It Comes to Book Sales, What Counts as Success Might Surprise You." *NPR.org*, September 19, 2015. https://www.npr.org/2015/09/19/441459103/when-it-comes-to-book-sales-what-counts-as-success-might-surprise-you.

Nelson, Daryl. "Why Are Young People So Obsessed with Becoming Famous?" *ConsumerAffairs*, January 21, 2013. https://www.consumeraffairs.com/news/why-are-young-people-so-obsessed-with-becoming-famous-012113.html.

Pew Research Center. "A Portrait of 'Generation Next.'" *US Politics* (blog), *Pew Research Center*,

January 9, 2007. https://www.pewresearch.org/politics/2007/01/09/a-portrait-of-generation-next/.

Polman, Evan, and Kyle J. Emich. "Decisions for Others Are More Creative Than Decisions for the Self." *Personality and Social Psychology Bulletin* 37, no. 4 (2011): 492-501. https://doi.org/10.1177/0146167211398362.

Renken, Elena. "Most Americans Are Lonely, and Our Workplace Culture May Not Be Helping." *NPR.org*, January 23, 2020. https://www.npr.org/sections/health-shots/2020/01/23/798676465/most-americans-are-lonely-and-our-workplace-culture-may-not-be-helping.

Robinson, Holly. "Why Do Writers Need Readers? Not for the Reason You Might Think." *HuffPost*, April 9, 2012. https://www.huffpost.com/entry/writers-readers_b_1262374.

ThermoSoft International Corporation. "'Making It' in America." Last modified January 1, 2018. https://www.thermosoft.com/en-US/blog/making-it-in-america.

Uhls, Yalda T. "Kids Want Fame More Than Anything" *HuffPost*, last modified April 26, 2012. https://www.huffpost.com/entry/kids-want-fame_b_1201935.

Vernon, Ferol. "What Makes a $100k Author: 8 Findings Every Author Should Know." *Written Word Media* (blog), June 7, 2017. https://www.writtenwordmedia.com/100k-author/.

Voysey, Sheridan. "Polls Say We're a Generation Seeking Fame. Here's Where That Will Lead Us." *Sheridan Voysey* (blog), February 18, 2020. https://sheridanvoysey.com/the-polls-say-were-a-generation-looking-for-fame-thats-a-problem/.

Chapter 4

Hill, Patrick L., and Nicholas A. Turiano. "Purpose in Life as a Predictor of Mortality Across Adulthood." *Psychological Science* 25, no. 7 (2014): 1482-1486. https://doi.org/10.1177/0956797614531799.

Hill, Patrick L., Nicholas A. Turiano, Daniel K. Mroczek, and Anthony L. Burrow. "The Value of a Purposeful Life: Sense of Purpose Predicts Greater Income and Net Worth." *Journal of Research in Personality* 65 (2016): 38-42. https://doi.org/10.1016/j.jrp.2016.07.003.

Kashdan, Todd B., and Patrick E. McKnight. "Commitment to a Purpose in Life: An Antidote to the Suffering by Individuals with Social Anxiety Disorder." *Emotion* 13, no. 6 (2013): 1150-1159. https://doi.org/10.1037/a0033278.

Kleftaras, George, and Evangelia Psarra. "Meaning in Life, Psychological Well-Being and Depressive Symptomatology: A Comparative Study." *Psychology* 3, no. 04 (2012): 337-345. https://doi.org/10.4236/psych.2012.34048.

Lukara, Alissa. "When Writers Get Depressed: An Interview with Eric Maisel About Creating Meaning with Your Writing." Transformational Writers. Accessed March 19, 2021. https://www.transformationalwriters.com/depression-writing-eric-maisel/.

McKnight, Patrick E., and Todd B. Kashdan. "Purpose in Life as a System That Creates and Sustains Health and Well-Being: An Integrative, Testable Theory." *Review of General Psychology* 13, no. 3 (2009): 242-251. https://doi.org/10.1037/a0017152.

Morin, Amy. "Science Says Finding Your Purpose Could Be the Key to Financial Success." *Inc.com*, March 28, 2017. https://www.inc.com/amy-morin/you-dont-have-to-choose-between-becoming-wealth-and-doing-something-meaningful-.html.

University College London. "Sense of Meaning and Purpose in Life Linked to Longer Lifespan." *UCL News* (blog), *UCL*, November 6, 2014. https://www.ucl.ac.uk/news/news-articles/1114/061114-longer-lifespan.

Chapter 5

Amabile, Teresa M. "Motivation and Creativity: Effects of Motivational Orientation on Creative Writers." *Journal of Personality and Social Psychology* 48, no. 2 (1985): 393-399. https://doi.org/10.1037/0022-3514.48.2.393.

Eisenberger, Robert, and Linda Shanock. "Rewards, Intrinsic Motivation, and Creativity: A Case Study of Conceptual and Methodological Isolation." *Creativity Research Journal* 15, no. 2 (2003): 121-130. https://doi:10.1207/s15326934crj152&3_02.

Karageorghis, Costas I., and Peter C. Terry. "Balance Intrinsic and Extrinsic Motivation for Success: An

Excerpt from *Inside Sport Psychology*." Human Kinetics. Accessed June 3, 2020. https://us.humankinetics.com/blogs/excerpt/balance-intrinsic-and-extrinsic-motivation-for-success.

Specter, Michael. "Drool." *The New Yorker*, last modified November 24, 2014. https://www.newyorker.com/magazine/2014/11/24/drool.

Chapter 6

Bright, Natalie. "Featured Writer on Wellness: Natalie Bright." *Writing and Wellness* (blog), July 11, 2018. https://writingandwellness.com/2018/07/11/featured-writer-on-wellness-natalie-bright/.

Chen, Jonlin, Masaru Ishii, Kristin L. Bater, Halley Darrach, David Liao, Pauline P. Huynh, Isabel P. Reh, Jason C. Nellis, Anisha R. Kumar, and Lisa E. Ishii. "Association Between the Use of Social Media and Photograph Editing Applications, Self-Esteem, and Cosmetic Surgery Acceptance." *JAMA Facial Plastic Surgery* 21, no. 5 (2019): 361-367. https://doi.org/10.1001/jamafacial.2019.0328.

Eckardt, Stephanie. "Anthony Hopkins Is Surprised How Popular His Paintings Are, Hasn't Been Asked Back 'Yet' for Westworld Season Two." *W Magazine*, January 11, 2017. https://www.wmagazine.com/story/anthony-hopkins-paintings-jeff-mitchum-westworld-season-two/.

Eckardt, Stephanie. "Val Kilmer Is Returning to Movies, But First He'd Like to Sell You a Painting from His First New York Art Show." *W Magazine*, June 2, 2017. https://www.wmagazine.com/story/val-kilmer-art-exhibit-new-york/.

Gibson, Jodi. "Dealing with Creative Guilt." *Jodi Gibson* (blog), January 10, 2017. https://jfgibson.com.au/creative-guilt/.

Ingram, Mona. "Featured Writer on Wellness: Mona Ingram." *Writing and Wellness* (blog), April 18, 2018. https://writingandwellness.com/2018/04/18/featured-writer-on-wellness-mona-ingram/.

Kizziar, Tim, as quoted in *Crazy Love: Overwhelmed by a Relentless God*, written by Francis Chan. Colorado Springs, Colorado: David C Cook, 2013.

Land, George. "TEDxTucson George Land The Failure of Success." YouTube. Filmed December 2011 at TEDxTucson, Tucson, AZ. Video, 13:06. https://www.youtube.com/watch?v=ZfKMq-rYtnc.

Land, George, and Beth Jarman. *Breakpoint and Beyond: Mastering the Future—Today*. New York: HarperCollins, 1993.

Ritter, Simone M., Rodica I. Damian, Dean K. Simonton, Rick B. Van Baaren, Madelijn Strick, Jeroen Derks, and Ap Dijksterhuis. "Diversifying Experiences Enhance Cognitive Flexibility." *Journal of Experimental Social Psychology* 48, no. 4 (2012): 961-964. https://doi.org/10.1016/j.jesp.2012.02.009.

Robinett, Lori. "Featured Writer on Wellness: Lori L. Robinett." *Writing and Wellness* (blog), April 25, 2018. https://writingandwellness.com/2018/04/25/featured-writer-on-wellness-lori-l-robinett/.

Shapiro, Stephen. "Do We Get Less Creative as We Age?" *Innovation Insights by Stephen Shapiro* (blog), *Stephen Shapiro*, last modified October 2, 2020. https://stephenshapiro.com/do-we-get-less-creative-as-we-age/.

Skillicorn, Nick. "Evidence That Children Become Less Creative over Time (and How to Fix It)." *Idea to Value*, August 5, 2016. https://www.ideatovalue.com/crea/nickskillicorn/2016/08/evidence-children-become-less-creative-time-fix/.

Yogman, Michael, Andrew Garner, Jeffrey Hutchinson, Kathy Hirsh-Pasek, and Roberta M. Golinkoff. "The Power of Play: A Pediatric Role in Enhancing Development in Young Children." *Pediatrics* 142, no. 3 (2018): e20182058. https://doi.org/10.1542/peds.2018-2058.

Chapter 7

Baikie, Karen A., and Kay Wilhelm. "Emotional and Physical Health Benefits of Expressive Writing." *Advances in Psychiatric Treatment* 11, no. 5 (2005): 338-346. https://doi.org/10.1192/apt.11.5.338.

Castrodale, Beth. "How to Write Your Way Through Loss and Grief." *Writing and Wellness* (blog), November 15, 2017. https://writingandwellness.com/2017/11/15/how-to-write-your-way-through-loss-and-grief/.

Hocker, Joyce. "Writing for Healing." *Psychology Today* (blog), March 17, 2018. https://www.psychologytoday.com/us/blog/building-resilience/201803/writing-healing.

Krpan, Katherine M., Ethan Kross, Marc G. Berman, Patricia J. Deldin, Mary K. Askren, and John

Jonides. "An Everyday Activity as a Treatment for Depression: The Benefits of Expressive Writing for People Diagnosed with Major Depressive Disorder." *Journal of Affective Disorders* 150, no. 3 (2013): 1148-1151. https://doi.org/10.1016/j.jad.2013.05.065.

Marcuse, Harold. "Lessons from the Diary of Anne Frank." Harold Marcuse, Professor of History at UC Santa Barbara. Last modified August 7, 2002. http://marcuse.faculty.history.ucsb.edu/present/13MarcuseAnneFrank.htm.

Munn, Rebecca Whitehead. "How Writing Taught Me to Live from My Heart." *Writing and Wellness* (blog), July 19, 2018. https://writingandwellness.com/2018/07/18/how-writing-taught-me-to-live-from-my-heart/.

Nannono, Jane. "How Writing a Book Helped Me Get to Know Myself." *Writing and Wellness* (blog), July 17, 2019. https://writingandwellness.com/2019/07/17/how-writing-a-book-helped-me-get-to-know-myself/.

O'Conner, Meg. "Evidence of the Healing Power of Expressive Writing." The Foundation for Art and Healing™. Last modified July 23, 2017. https://artandhealing.org/evidence-of-the-healing-power-of-expressive-writing/.

Olmstead, Rebecca. "In Writing, I Found the Purpose in My Pain." *Writing and Wellness* (blog), June 3, 2020. https://writingandwellness.com/2020/06/03/in-writing-i-found-the-purpose-in-my-pain/.

Pachankis, John E., and Marvin R. Goldfried. "Expressive Writing for Gay-Related Stress: Psychosocial Benefits and Mechanisms Underlying Improvement." *Journal of Consulting and Clinical Psychology* 78, no. 1 (2010): 98-110. https://doi.org/10.1037/a0017580.

Pennebaker, James W. "Expressive Writing in Psychological Science." *Perspectives on Psychological Science* 13, no. 2 (2017): 226-229. https://doi.org/10.1177/1745691617707315.

Pennebaker, James W., and Sandra K. Beall. "Confronting a Traumatic Event: Toward an Understanding of Inhibition and Disease." *Journal of Abnormal Psychology* 95, no. 3 (1986): 274-281. https://doi.org/10.1037//0021-843x.95.3.274.

Pennebaker, James W., and Joshua M. Smyth. *Opening Up by Writing It Down: How Expressive Writing Improves Health and Eases Emotional Pain.* 3rd ed. New York: Guilford Publications, 2016.

Petrie, Keith J., Iris Fontanilla, Mark G. Thomas, Roger J. Booth, and James W. Pennebaker. "Effect of Written Emotional Expression on Immune Function in Patients with Human Immunodeficiency Virus Infection: A Randomized Trial." *Psychosomatic Medicine* 66, no. 2 (2004): 272-275. https://doi.org/10.1097/01.psy.0000116782.49850.d3.

Robinson, Hayley, Paul Jarrett, Kavita Vedhara, and Elizabeth Broadbent. "The Effects of Expressive Writing Before or After Punch Biopsy on Wound Healing." *Brain, Behavior, and Immunity* 61 (2017): 217-227. https://doi.org/10.1016/j.bbi.2016.11.025.

Schroder, Hans S., Tim P. Moran, and Jason S. Moser. "The Effect of Expressive Writing on the Error-Related Negativity Among Individuals with Chronic Worry." *Psychophysiology* 55, no. 2 (2017): e12990. https://doi.org/10.1111/psyp.12990.

Shen, Lujun, Lei Yang, Jing Zhang, and Meng Zhang. "Benefits of Expressive Writing in Reducing Test Anxiety: A Randomized Controlled Trial in Chinese Samples." *PLOS ONE* 13, no. 2 (2018): e0191779. https://doi.org/10.1371/journal.pone.0191779.

Simon, Jo Ann. "How Writing to Heal Led to a Touching Story of Love." *Writing and Wellness* (blog), September 18, 2018. https://writingandwellness.com/2018/09/05/how-writing-to-heal-led-to-a-touching-story-of-love/.

Smyth, Joshua M., Arthur A. Stone, Adam Hurewitz, and Alan Kaell. "Effects of Writing About Stressful Experiences on Symptom Reduction in Patients with Asthma or Rheumatoid Arthritis." *JAMA* 281, no. 14 (1999): 1304. https://doi:10.1001/jama.281.14.1304.

Somlo, Patty. "How Fiction Can Help You Find Peace with Your Past." *Writing and Wellness* (blog), May 9, 2018. https://writingandwellness.com/2018/05/09/how-fiction-can-help-you-find-peace-with-your-past/.

Stanton, Annette L., Sharon Danoff-Burg, Lisa A. Sworowski, Charlotte A. Collins, Ann D. Branstetter, Alicia Rodriguez-Hanley, Sarah B. Kirk, and Jennifer L. Austenfeld. "Randomized, Controlled Trial of

Written Emotional Expression and Benefit Finding in Breast Cancer Patients." *Journal of Clinical Oncology* 20, no. 20 (2002): 4160-4168. https://doi:10.1200/jco.2002.08.521.

Tonarelli, Annalisa, Chiara Cosentino, Diletta Artioli, Stefania Borciani, Elena Camurri, Barbara Colombo, Antonio D'Errico, Liana Lelli, Laura Lodini, and Giovanna Artioli. "Expressive Writing. A Tool to Help Health Workers. Research Project on the Benefits of Expressive Writing." *Acta Biomedica* 88, Suppl. 5 (2017): 13–21. https://doi:10.23750/abm.v88i5-S.6877.

Chapter 8

"Americans Spend 4 Years of Their Lives 'Escaping Reality'." *New York Post*, July 3, 2017. https://nypost.com/2017/07/03/americans-spend-4-years-of-their-lives-escaping-reality/.

Birkwood, Ilene. "Featured Writer on Wellness: Ilene Birkwood." *Writing and Wellness* (blog), July 6, 2017. https://writingandwellness.com/2017/07/06/featured-writer-on-wellness-ilene-birkwood/.

Bushman, Brad J. "Does Venting Anger Feed or Extinguish the Flame? Catharsis, Rumination, Distraction, Anger, and Aggressive Responding." *Personality and Social Psychology Bulletin* 28, no. 6 (2002): 724-731. https://doi.org/10.1177/0146167202289002.

Greene, Graham. *Ways of Escape*. New York: Random House, 2011.

Hammond, Claudia. "Does Reading Fiction Make Us Better People?" *BBC Future* (blog), *BBC*, June 2, 2019. https://www.bbc.com/future/article/20190523-does-reading-fiction-make-us-better-people.

Hart Research Associates. *Raising the Bar: Employers' Views on College Learning in the Wake of the Economic Downturn*. 2010. https://www.aacu.org/sites/default/files/files/LEAP/2009_EmployerSurvey.pdf.

Johnson, Dan R. "Transportation into a Story Increases Empathy, Prosocial Behavior, and Perceptual Bias Toward Fearful Expressions." *Personality and Individual Differences* 52, no. 2 (2012): 150-155. https://doi.org/10.1016/j.paid.2011.10.005.

Ohno, Shiroh. "Internet Ecapism and Addiction Among Japanese Senior High School Students."

International Journal of Culture and Mental Health 9, no. 4 (2016): 399-406. https://doi.org/10.1080/17542863.2016.1226911.

Raine, Kai. "When the Story Refuses to Be Abandoned." *Writing and Wellness* (blog), May 18, 2018. https://writingandwellness.com/2018/05/16/when-the-story-refuses-to-be-abandoned/.

Schouten, Werner. "The Overlooked Consequence of Phone Use: Self-Escapism." *LinkedIn* (blog), July 16, 2018. https://www.linkedin.com/pulse/overlooked-consequence-phone-use-self-escapism-werner-schouten/.

Secora, Sara. "My 10-Year Struggle to Get My Story Published." *Writing and Wellness* (blog), April 10, 2019. https://writingandwellness.com/2019/04/10/my-10-year-struggle-to-get-my-story-published/.

Tamir, Diana I., Andrew B. Bricker, David Dodell-Feder, and Jason P. Mitchell. "Reading Fiction and Reading Minds: The Role of Simulation in the Default Network." *Social Cognitive and Affective Neuroscience* 11, no. 2 (2016): 215-224. https://doi.org/10.1093/scan/nsv114.

Weiland, K. M. "4 Ways Writing Improves Your Relationship with Yourself." *Helping Writers Become Authors* (blog), April 20, 2020. https://www.helpingwritersbecomeauthors.com/how-writing-improves-your-relationship-with-yourself/.

"Writing: A Ticket to Work . . . Or a Ticket Out." National Writing Project. Accessed November 26, 2020. https://archive.nwp.org/cs/public/print/resource/2540.

Wood, Erick Graham. "COLUMN: Escapism Is Proof Americans Are Unhappy." *The Utah Statesman*, February 18, 2019. https://usustatesman.com/column-escapism-is-proof-americans-are-unhappy/.

Chapter 9

Acheson, Ian. "Writing to Discover Truth . . . and Yourself." *ACFW | American Christian Fiction Writers* (blog), July 14, 2016. https://www.acfw.com/blog/writing-to-discover-truth-and-yourself/.

Craft, Kathryn. "Seeking Truth in Fiction." *Writer Unboxed* (blog), January 14, 2019. https://writerunboxed.com/2019/01/10/seeking-truth-in-fiction/.

Langwell, Crissi. "Writing a Novel About the True-Life Loss of a Child." *Writing and Wellness* (blog), May 8, 2019. https://writingandwellness.com/2019/05/08/writing-a-novel-about-the-true-life-loss-of-a-child/.

Loehr, Jim. *The Only Way to Win: How Building Character Drives Higher Achievement and Greater Fulfillment in Business and Life*. London: Hachette UK, 2012.

Mansfield, Elaine. "Grieving Widow Turns Feelings of Loss into a Touching Memoir." *Writing and Wellness* (blog), October 2, 2014. https://writingandwellness.com/2014/10/02/grieving-widow-turns-feelings-of-loss-into-a-touching-memoir/.

Noblitt, Bill. "Are the Big Questions Still Relevant." *Stetson Today* (blog), *Stetson University*, June 5, 2015. https://www.stetson.edu/today/2015/06/are-the-big-questions-still-relevant/.

Rapp, Adam. "Gina Gionfriddo, Rolin Jones and Adam Rapp." By Sarah Hart. *The American Theatre Reader: Essays and Conversations from American Theatre Magazine*, edited by the staff of *American Theatre Magazine*, 578–588. New York: Theatre Communications Group, 2009.

Reiter, Kimberly D. S. "On Being Human." *Stetson Today* (blog), *Stetson University*, July 31, 2015. https://www.stetson.edu/today/2015/07/being-human/.

Stockton, Amanda. "Writing Truth in Fiction." *Batwords Media* (blog), April 15, 2020. https://www.batwordsmedia.com/post/writing-truth-in-fiction.

Chapter 10

Dolan, Eric W. "Study: Performing Artists Who Suffered in Childhood Tend to Have More Intense Creative Experiences." *PsyPost*, May 5, 2018. https://www.psypost.org/2018/05/study-performing-artists-suffered-childhood-tend-intense-creative-experiences-51152.

Kabrich, Mary Avery. "Overcoming Dyslexia to Write an Award-Winning Novel." *Writing and Wellness* (blog), January 9, 2019. https://writingandwellness.com/2019/01/09/overcoming-dyslexia-to-write-an-award-winning-novel/.

Sienkiewicz, Linda K. "Women Need to Tell Their Stories Without Shame." *Writing and Wellness* (blog), June 21, 2016. https://writingandwellness.com/2016/06/21/women-need-to-tell-their-stories-without-shame/.

Somlo, Patty. "How Fiction Can Help You Find Peace with Your Past." *Writing and Wellness* (blog), May 9, 2018. https://writingandwellness.com/2018/05/09/how-fiction-can-help-you-find-peace-with-your-past/.

Starr, Michelle. "Scientists Have Found a Strong Link Between a Terrible Childhood and Being Intensely Creative." *ScienceAlert*, May 8, 2018. https://www.sciencealert.com/childhood-adversity-linked-to-intense-creative-process.

Thomson, Paula, and S. V. Jaque. "Childhood Adversity and the Creative Experience in Adult Professional Performing Artists." *Frontiers in Psychology* 9 (2018): 111. https://doi.org/10.3389/fpsyg.2018.00111.

Chapter 11

Carlyle, Josh. "How Essay Writing Can Enhance Your Critical Thinking Skills." *American Board Blog*, *American Board for Certification of Teacher Excellence*, November 13, 2018. https://www.americanboard.org/blog/how-essay-writing-can-enhance-your-critical-thinking-skills/.

Haave, Neil. "Developing Students' Thinking by Writing." Tomorrow's Professor Postings, Stanford University. Last modified December 2015. https://tomprof.stanford.edu/posting/1472.

Lotze, Martin, Katharina Erhard, Nicola Neumann, Simon B. Eickhoff, and Robert Langner. "Neural Correlates of Verbal Creativity: Differences in Resting-State Functional Connectivity Associated with Expertise in Creative Writing." *Frontiers in Human Neuroscience* 8 (2014): 516. https://doi.org/10.3389/fnhum.2014.00516.

McCullough, David. "The Title Always Comes Last." By Bruce Cole. National Endowment for the Humanities. Last modified 2003. https://www.neh.gov/about/awards/jefferson-lecture/david-mccullough-biography.

Menary, Richard. "Writing as Thinking." *Language Sciences* 29, no. 5 (September 2007): 621-632. https://doi.org/10.1016/j.langsci.2007.01.005.

Quitadamo, Ian J., and Martha J. Kurtz. "Learning to Improve: Using Writing to Increase Critical Thinking Performance in General Education Biology." *CBE—Life Sciences Education* 6, no. 2 (2007): 140-154. https://doi.org/10.1187/cbe.06-11-0203.

Randolph, Patrick T. "Using Creative Writing as a Bridge to Enhance Academic Writing." Paper presented at Michigan Teachers of English to Speakers of Other Languages Conference, Kalamazoo, Michigan, October 2011.

Zimmer, Carl. "This Is Your Brain on Writing." *The New York Times*, June 20, 2014. https://www.nytimes.com/2014/06/19/science/researching-the-brain-of-writers.html.

Chapter 12

"5 Journaling Exercises to Get to Know Yourself a Lot Better." *Manhattan Mental Health Counseling* (blog), last modified October 24, 2019. https://manhattanmentalhealthcounseling.com/5-journaling-exercises-to-get-to-know-yourself-a-lot-better/.

Böckler, Anne, Lukas Herrmann, Fynn-Mathis Trautwein, Tom Holmes, and Tania Singer. "Know Thy Selves: Learning to Understand Oneself Increases the Ability to Understand Others." *Journal of Cognitive Enhancement* 1, no. 2 (2017): 197-209. https://doi.org/10.1007/s41465-017-0023-6.

Dao, Julie C. "Knowing Yourself Better Through Writing." *Pub(lishing) Crawl* (blog), June 15, 2018. https://www.publishingcrawl.com/2018/06/15/knowing-yourself-better-through-writing/.

Dubus, Andre, III. *Townie: A Memoir*. New York: W. W. Norton & Company, 2011.

Grason, Sandy. *Journalution: Journal Writing to Awaken Your Inner Voice, Heal Your Life, and Manifest Your Dreams*. Novato, California: New World Library, 2010.

Gressel, Josh. "Why What I Admire in You Also Says Something About Me." *Psychology Today* (blog), August 6, 2017. https://www.psychologytoday.com/us/blog/putting-psyche-back-psychotherapy/201708/why-what-i-admire-in-you-also-says-something-about-me.

"Literature and Medicine: Why Do We Care?" *The Lancet* 385, no. 9963 (2015): 90. https://doi.org/10.1016/S0140-6736(15)60004-6.

Nikolova, Niia. "Want to Be Happier? Try Getting to Know Yourself." *The Conversation*, January 14, 2019. https://theconversation.com/want-to-be-happier-try-getting-to-know-yourself-109451.

Pushkar, Robert G. "Andre Dubus III: Cave Art." *The Writer* (blog), updated October 21, 2018. https://www.writermag.com/writing-inspiration/author-interviews/andre-dubus-iii-cave-art/.

Svitorka, Tomas. "Knowing Yourself Is a Cornerstone of Success and Happiness." *Tomas Svitorka* (blog), May 21, 2017. https://tomassvitorka.com/knowing-yourself/.

Tartakovsky, Margarita. "5 Ways to Get to Know Yourself Better." *PsychCentral* (blog), August 6, 2012. https://psychcentral.com/blog/5-ways-to-get-to-know-yourself-better/.

Thackray, Gail. "Your Soul Purpose Reflected in the People You Admire." *Gail Thackray* (blog), last modified March 11, 2019. https://www.gailthackray.com/post/your-soul-purpose-reflected-in-the-people-you-admire.

Ward, Emma. "Insightful Quotes from Willa Cather." *Author Quotes* (blog), *Literary Ladies Guide: Inspiration for Readers and Writers from Classic Women Authors*, May 26, 2017. https://www.literaryladiesguide.com/author-quotes/insightful-quotes-willa-cather/.

Weston, Gabriel. "Developing Judgment, Not Being Judgmental." *The Lancet* 385, no. 9963 (2015): 108-109. https://doi.org/10.1016/S0140-6736(15)60010-1.

Chapter 13

Harvard Health Publishing. "In Praise of Gratitude." Harvard Medical School. Last modified June 5, 2019. https://www.health.harvard.edu/newsletter_article/in-praise-of-gratitude.

Hearn, Stuart. "Your Employees Feel Underappreciated. Here's What You Can Do to Fix It." Business.com. Last modified June 29, 2017. https://www.business.com/articles/stuart-hearn-improving-employee-performance-through-recognition/.

Langwell, Crissi. "Answering the Hard Questions About Life As a Writer." *Crissi Langwell* (blog), October 16, 2019. https://crissilangwell.com/2019/10/16/answering-the-hard-questions-about-life-as-a-writer/.

Weiss, Lauren. "15 Writers on Writing." *The New York Public Library* (blog), October 10, 2015. https://www.nypl.org/blog/2015/10/20/15-writers-writing.

Chapter 14

Breslin, Susannah. "Why You Shouldn't Be A Writer." *Forbes*, June 12, 2012. https://www.forbes.com/sites/susannahbreslin/2012/06/12/why-you-shouldnt-be-a-writer/#1861bd2930a6.

Gowen, Karen Jones. "Featured Writer on Wellness: Karen Jones Gowen." *Writing and Wellness* (blog), September 10, 2015. https://writingandwellness.com/2015/09/10/featured-writer-on-wellness-karen-jones-gowen/.

Steiner, Susie. "Top Five Regrets of the Dying." *The Guardian*, February 1, 2012. https://www.theguardian.com/lifeandstyle/2012/feb/01/top-five-regrets-of-the-dying.

Chapter 15

No references.

Chapter 16

"A Person Has Two Reasons for Doing Anything: A Good Reason and the Real Reason." *Quote Investigator* (blog), last modified May 22, 2014. https://quoteinvestigator.com/2014/03/26/two-reasons/#note-8492-1.

Durayappah-Harrison, Adoree. "The Real Reason Some of Us Are Chronically Late." *Psychology Today* (blog), November 14, 2014. https://www.psychologytoday.com/us/blog/thriving101/201411/the-real-reason-some-us-are-chronically-late.

Acknowledgments

My sincere gratitude to:

P. J. Dempsey, for her invaluable assistance as editor and coach and for her belief in this book and its message. My deepest gratitude!

Sara Letourneau, for her careful and thorough copyedit and proofread. Thanks for reviewing everything so carefully!

My cover designer at Damonza, who has maintained a cohesive look among my (now) three nonfiction books for writers.

The writers who agreed to share their stories in this book—your openness and humility inspire me and help all of us writers defeat our demons together.

All those who subscribe to my motivational blog, *Writing and Wellness*—thank you for your ongoing interest and support of my mission to help writers live their best creative lives. I couldn't do this without you!

My family, particularly my mother, for continuing to support my writing endeavors. A writer never grows out of her need for this support, and I'm grateful.

About the Author

Colleen M. Story inspires writers to overcome modern-day challenges and find creative fulfillment in their work. Her last nonfiction release, *Your Writing Matters*, helps writers overcome self-doubt and determine once and for all where writing fits in their lives. Her previous release, *Writer Get Noticed!*, was a gold-medal winner in the Reader's Favorite Book Awards and a first-place winner in the Reader Views Literary Awards. *Overwhelmed Writer Rescue* was named Book by Book Publicity's Best Writing/Publishing Book in 2018 and was an Amazon best seller. Her novel, *Loreena's Gift*, was a Foreword Reviews' INDIES Book of the Year Awards winner, among others. Her next novel, *The Beached Ones*, is forthcoming in the spring of 2022.

With over 20 years as a freelance writer in the health and wellness industry, Colleen has authored thousands of articles for publications like "Healthline" and "Women's Health;" worked with high-profile clients like Gerber Baby Products and Kellogg's; and ghostwritten books on back pain, nutrition, and cancer recovery.

She frequently serves as a workshop leader and motivational speaker, where she helps attendees remove mental and emotional blocks and tap into their unique creative powers.

A lifelong musician, Colleen plays the French horn in her local symphony and pit orchestras. When not writing, she's walking, reading, practicing yoga, listening to music, and exploring the beautiful Northwest.

For more information, see her websites at Writing and Wellness (writingandwellness.com), Life and Everything After (lifeandeverythingafter.com), and her author website (colleenmstory.com), or follow her on Twitter (@ colleen_m_story) and YouTube.

www.ingramcontent.com/pod-product-compliance
Lightning Source LLC
Chambersburg PA
CBHW070542010526
44118CB00012B/1187